WILDLIFE GARDENING

RHODA NOTTRIDGE

THE CROWOOD PRESS

First published in 2009 by
The Crowood Press Ltd
Ramsbury, Marlborough
Wiltshire SN8 2HR

www.crowood.com

British Library Cataloguing-in-Publication Data

A catalogue record for this book is available from the British Library.

ISBN 978 1 84797 098 5

All photographs are by Rhoda Nottridge, with the exception of page 62 (Dawn Lewis), page 64 (A.J. Hunt) and page 73 (Sally Cunningham)

Thanks to the following for permission to photograph their gardens:
Mr and Mrs Curry's Wildlife Garden, Brighton (front cover and page 26);
Wol and Sue Staines, Glen Chantry Garden, Essex (page 72);
Bridgette Saunders' Garden, Brighton (page 106)

Illustrations by Caroline Pratt

Dedication
For my father, Harold Edgar Nottridge (1912–2008)

Typeset by Florence Production Ltd, Stoodleigh, Devon

Printed and bound in Singapore by Craft Print International

Contents

CHAPTER 1

Getting to know your garden

A garden, however small or large, is a joy to many of us. The more one watches things growing and changing through the seasons, the more one notices that a garden is not just a composition of plants and trees, but a wider tapestry into which are woven a myriad of creatures. From the smallest micro-organisms that keep the soil healthy to the snuffling sounds of the largest visiting mammals, a garden is not just about plants, it is also about wildlife.

We cannot garden in isolation from the wildlife that lives and breathes in it. As we learn about growing and keeping plants flourishing in a garden, it becomes clear that we need to work with and not against garden wildlife. For some years, it was commonly believed that a garden was an area to be conquered by its owners, with any unwanted creatures being exterminated, and as a result, gardens were beginning to lose all natural balance.

At last, the thinking on how to keep a healthy, happy garden is changing. Gardening with wildlife in mind is not a new idea but one that has gained a huge amount of momentum in recent times. The premise is really quite simple: that by caring for the wildlife in our gardens, we create a balanced environment that is good for our plants, good for the wildlife, and good for the planet.

A wildlife garden also adds a huge amount to our enjoyment of gardens and gardening. It opens up our understanding and observation of the many, varied creatures that inhabit this space. Our eyes are opened to other worlds that go on in the garden and all around us. The more we learn about what lives in our gardens and what potential these

Wildflowers can be every bit as charming as cultivated varieties and are often more beneficial to wildlife.

creatures hold for creating a thriving community of wildlife, the more pleasure we can gain from knowing we benefit not just ourselves but also the world at large.

We usually think of our gardens with a strong sense of ownership and often pride. This belies the fact that actually we are merely tenants on this earth and that we share it with very many other creatures. With our ever-increasing understanding of the importance of an ecological balance in the world, and the consequences of not keeping this balance, allowing and encouraging wildlife to live alongside us makes perfect sense.

One of the great joys of gardening with wildlife in mind is that it opens up not one new world, but many. We may start by noticing the larger creatures that visit the garden, such as mammals and birds. Then we start to see the smaller creatures, such as the butterflies and the bees, until we begin to realize that everything is alive and sustaining other life. This knowledge can begin to alter our whole perspective on life. Even when a living thing in the garden dies or decays, it is still part of a greater cycle of life that affects us all. If we garden responsibly we can contribute a great deal to keeping this fascinating cycle of life going, while deeply improving our own understanding and quality of living.

Wildlife requires a variety of habitats, each of which creates a community of living creatures, all dependent on each other for food. Most gardens offer a small number of habitats but if several gardens are next to each other, the combined total may create sufficient diversity of species to support a community.

In your individual garden, the more variety you offer, the more species from this community will be attracted to live in or visit your garden and so the more diversity you are supporting in wildlife. We can also try to help with biodiversity on the planet. Biodiversity means not just supporting a variety of organisms and creatures but also means helping to keep a genetic variation alive in the species and also the plants that we might choose for our garden.

The best way to garden successfully and in a way that will improve rather than damage the environment is to learn what will and won't work in your specific garden. This means working with your garden site and soil, rather than trying to grow the wrong types of plants in the wrong areas.

So the first questions to work out are: which parts of the garden are sunny or shady? Which areas remain moist, and which dry out quickly? What

These attractive plants were found growing in the shingle on a beach. From looking at the local conditions, the gardener can discover what similar types of plant will thrive in their garden.

kind of soil does the garden have? How sheltered or exposed is the site? Starting to recognize some of these factors will mean you can anticipate what sort of difficulties might occur in the garden and what you can do to work with instead of against them.

The first area to consider is the aspect of the garden. This means the way the sun moves around it during the day. Throughout the year, the position of the sun will vary, as it is higher in the sky in the summer and lower in the winter. If you have a garden that is new to you, it may be worth making a rough note of which areas have sunshine or not through the first year. A south-facing garden will be the sunniest and a north-facing garden the coldest but depending on the size of the garden and the way the shadows of the house and surrounding buildings fall, other areas may also be in shade.

So the north side of a garden will be in permanent shade all year round and will not heat up as much as the rest of the garden. You may not have garden areas on all sides, but the east side will get morning sun and the west side afternoon and evening sun. A south-facing garden will get the most sun all day and be warmest.

How the sun falls on the house itself is also important, as the walls on the south side will warm up quickly and stay warmer all year, so plants requiring warmth should be planted on this side. This is the best place for summer flowering plants and as it will dry out more quickly, it is also suited to plants that like drier conditions, such as lavenders and rosemary, which do well in Mediterranean climes. The north side will always be cold and shady, so choose plants for this side that would naturally prefer colder, shadier conditions, such as woodland plants.

Trees and tall hedges will also cast shadows that should be noted. The ground underneath them will be dry in the summer if they are deciduous, and dry all year if evergreen. This means that underplanting in these areas needs to be with plants that like dry shade, or in the case of deciduous trees, with plants that have flowered before the tree canopy is out, such as spring bulbs.

If the garden slopes, there can be other areas that will be affected. A slope down towards a hedge or wall or a dip in a slope will create a shady area

*Getting to know which plants will grow where will make for better gardening; Busy Lizzies (*Impatiens walleriana*) will be happy with just a little sun each day, so can be grown in a semi-shaded spot.*

that will become a frost pocket, so anything growing in that area needs to be completely frost hardy. A slope facing away from the sun will be cold and shady.

Exposure to wind will affect the growth of many plants, causing wind burn, which can look a little like frost damage. The wind dries out plants, preventing them from being able to transpire properly through their leaves, so ultimately they will die from a lack of water. However, a little knowledge can greatly improve a plant's chance of survival in a windy environment. There are two types of action that can be taken. One is to create permeable shelter belts using hedging, which is good for wildlife and good for the garden. The other tactic is to become familiar with plants that can cope well with wind.

This can be done by starting to look around at the plants and trees that grow well on exposed sites, and also becoming familiar with adaptations that plants make to help them cope with dry or windier conditions, such as having very leathery or narrow leaves, which are not so badly affected by the conditions.

Other factors to consider are the more general aspects that affect gardens in your area, such as the prevailing climate. This will affect rainfall, which will in turn affect the humidity in the garden. A very moist, wet garden will encourage mould on plants that prefer dry conditions but will be ideal for plants such as ferns. The seasonal temperature will be very important in deciding the progress of many plants as all plants have a minimum and maximum

We can learn a lot about our gardens by the plants that thrive in them. Buttercups, for example, are often an indication of damp soil.

to wildlife. When making changes in a garden, try not to disturb any wildlife that already lives in the garden, and keep areas of shelter available, so that small animals can scuttle off to these places while any improvements are being carried out.

Probably the first thing to consider is the garden's aspect, followed by a proper assessment of your soil type, texture and pH. Details about this are in Chapter 2. Then you can start to think about the design, if any, that you have in the garden and (after reading this book) features that you might like to include both for wildlife and also for your own use.

You might even want to consider measuring the garden and making a scale map of it on graph paper. You can then use tracing or thin overlay paper to try out lots of different designs. If you are planning hard landscaping features this will help you get an idea of the quantity of materials you may require for a specific project.

There are some basic principles that most garden designs will follow. The scale of the garden is important, in that the plants, trees and any garden features need to be in proportion with each other; they will also look strange if they are not suited to the size of the garden. So for example, a small garden will look best with a small garden tree, not one that will occupy all the light in the garden and grow as high as the house.

It is good to vary the look of a garden by bringing in plants with a range of textures and colours, shapes and heights, so that they will create contrasts around

temperature range in which they will flourish. Your garden will also have a microclimate. For example, if it is slightly warmer where you live than in the region generally, this can be used to push the boundaries of what it is possible to grow in your garden.

DESIGNING A GARDEN WITH WILDLIFE IN MIND

Redesigning an entire garden is a major task and may not be necessary. However, incorporating a few elements into the garden little by little will have the least impact on existing wildlife but will nonetheless make your garden far more attractive

Wildlife gardens suit naturalistic planting schemes, so using a plant such as ivy to cover unsightly areas provides both shelter and food for birds and other wildlife.

Flowers, grasses, shrubs and trees will all combine to create lush growth within which wildlife can survive.

Wildlife gardens tend to suit naturalistic shaping of items such as paths and ponds but it is also possible to cater for wildlife and keep one area, such as a parterre, strictly designed and controlled, if this is an image that is wanted.

Another way is just to develop the garden intuitively, making one change at a time and seeing what impact each change has on the garden. If you feel stuck for ideas, go and visit any wildlife gardens that are open to the public. Many private gardens are also opened occasionally to the public for charity fund-raising, such as those open in the National Garden Scheme; many of these are inspirational for gathering ideas for designing your own garden. Most of the possibilities for a domestic garden can also be put into practice on an allotment or a community garden.

The Royal Horticultural Society has also recently been involved in encouraging schools to give over some of their grounds to wildlife gardening. If a school near you has an open day, it is well worth taking a look at some of the many inspirational ideas schools can use to enthuse children. It makes a great deal of sense to give children a sense of familiarity with wildlife, wild plants and gardening, which has been very much lost in the last few decades. Some of the ideas the schools are incorporating can also be used in a small back garden and will inspire any children in the household.

Indeed, planning a wildlife garden also means considering who will be using the garden and making sure it will function well for all concerned. If you are a family with young children, this may mean having a bog garden rather than a pond, but older children will love getting to know pond life in its many forms. Keeping areas of the garden or grass undisturbed for wildlife may mean making other parts more appealing to children. For gardens used only by adults, there need be fewer concerns about safety and in this quieter environment the amount of wildlife it is possible to encourage is quite astounding. Some of the smaller creatures, of course, like insects, will not be concerned by the presence of people, just so long as they have the right plants to survive on.

The fundamental aspect of selecting plants for a wildlife garden is to choose ideally native plants that will provide food and or shelter for wildlife.

the garden. It is also good to have some unifying factors that appear repeatedly through the garden, to bring it all together so that it does not feel too muddled. This may be done by using the same shapes around the garden, or limiting the palette of colours used or by making sure that the materials used throughout the garden are the same, so that, for example, the garden seats and a pergola are all made from recycled wood, rather than a mixture of materials.

Building a wildlife hotel is simple and provides insects with shelter and a place to overwinter, compensating for their loss of natural habitats.

pond, some sort of water will be vital for many types of creatures and will introduce a whole new range of wildlife into your garden.

There are wider considerations to be made when planning a wildlife garden than simply your own plot. Animals do not live by the artificial boundaries that we have created and therefore our wildlife gardens cannot be seen in isolation from other wildlife areas around us. Many animals travel a considerable distance to find food and shelter and often use what are called 'wildlife corridors' to make these journeys.

A wildlife corridor means an area that is sufficiently sheltered to enable animals to travel undetected along them to move between areas. For example, if your next-door neighbour has hedging along the bottom of their garden, you can add a mixed hedge along the bottom of your garden and leave some gaps between the two boundaries. This way, animals can move along without being seen. There is some debate about how successful wildlife corridors are but the more areas that allow wildlife to flourish, the better.

For birds, the meaning of a wildlife corridor can be quite different. As we have many birds that fly long distances to breeding and feeding grounds, depending on the seasons, hedgerows and other areas around wildlife corridors allow them to stop, feed and drink alongside the permanent residents. Wildlife corridors can also act as shelter belts to lessen the impact of prevailing winds on the garden.

Adding at least one tree, if at all possible, is a very important feature for birds and many other creatures and will create height and a focal point to a garden. With wildlife in mind, choosing plants also means creating a good balance of contrasting colours, shapes and growth habits. A good wildlife garden is also a haven in all seasons, so it is well worth making sure that there are plants and flowers throughout the year.

Lastly, without water, there can be no life at all, so no matter whether it is an old bucket or a large

A log pile will create a place of shelter for wildlife during the winter months and a home for insects.

DESIGN FEATURES FOR A WILDLIFE GARDEN

The following is a list of some of the features that are worth considering when designing a garden for wildlife. These features can be adapted to the size of the garden. Even a patio can include much of the planting, in pots. Don't forget to add elements that are strictly for humans, such as garden seating, paths, sheds and greenhouses.

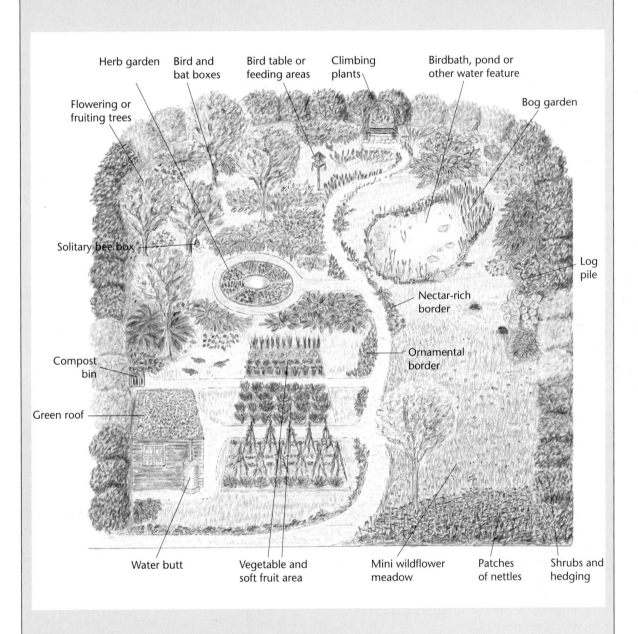

Herb garden
Bird and bat boxes
Bird table or feeding areas
Climbing plants
Birdbath, pond or other water feature
Bog garden
Flowering or fruiting trees
Solitary bee box
Log pile
Nectar-rich border
Compost bin
Ornamental border
Green roof
Water butt
Vegetable and soft fruit area
Mini wildflower meadow
Patches of nettles
Shrubs and hedging

CHAPTER 2

Understanding the earth

Gardening for wildlife begins beneath the feet – not with the plants, but with the soil that supports the plants. Healthy, balanced soil means healthy plants and there are several things that can be done to improve the soil.

Within the soil live legions of mini-beasts, from the helpful worm, which aerates the soil and breaks down organic matter, to many micro-organisms that are so small they cannot be seen with the naked eye. All of these creatures are vital in creating soil that will produce healthy plants.

Your first task as a wildlife gardener is to find out what type of soil you have in your garden. Soil is described as topsoil and subsoil. Plants grow in the topsoil, which may contain a lot of sand, clay, chalk, silt or be a very good loam, which is the ideal type of soil. What kind of soil you have depends on where you live.

SOIL TYPES

There are five main types of soil. The particles that make them up vary in size and this in turn affects the soil's ability to hold on to water and nutrients. So this will affect how the soil needs to be treated.

If you feel you need to know more about the subsoil, you can dig a test pit, about 1m wide and 60cm deep, to see what strata lie beneath the topsoil and also to establish what kind of water drainage the soil allows.

Rhododendrons thrive on acid soils, so if a lot of them grow nearby this may be an indication that the soil type in your garden is acidic.

Clay soil

Clay soil can be very rich and fertile but it is made up of very small particles that stick together, making it heavy and hard to work. Clay soil is slow to warm up in the spring, which means plants may get off to a slow start. In summer droughts, the soil can harden up so it is very hard to work; if you consider that bricks are made out of baked clay, the soil can feel as hard as bricks. The soil doesn't have a good capacity for drainage, because of the way the soil sticks together. It can also suffer from compaction.

To improve the soil and drainage, add composted bark at about one wheelbarrow-full per square metre. The bark adds structure to the soil. To improve the drainage and structure further you can add grit. Well-rotted mushroom compost, which is alkaline, is good for balancing this acidic soil and is lighter than ordinary compost.

HOW TO TEST SOIL TEXTURE

The easiest way to test and establish what soil type you have in the garden is to touch it. Take a handful of soil, from about a trowel's depth. (Surface soil may include too much organic matter.) Add water if the soil is dry and then shape it into a ball, which may remind you of making mud pies as a child.

If the soil is clay, it easily goes into a solid ball and has a sticky feel to it, rather as if you were making pottery. If you rub it, it polishes up and shines.

Sandy soil feels gritty in texture. It will not readily make a ball shape, tending to fall apart in your hands.

A good loam can be rolled into ball and doesn't feel gritty.

Chalky or limestone soil

Shallow chalk soil is free draining but as a result, nutrients can be lost from the soil quite fast as many seep out with the water. It benefits from a good thick annual mulch of organic matter, so will be happy to receive plenty of well-rotted manure, leaf mould, or garden compost. If the soil is a mixture of clay and chalk, it is better to treat the soil as for clay and improve the soil structure.

Sandy or silty soils

The great thing about a sandy soil is that it is very light to work and warms up well in the spring. Just as grains of sand slip through your fingers, so sandy soil drains so well that nutrients slip through it very quickly too, making it hard to improve. Organic matter can be added but will quickly seep through the soil, so there is no need to dig it in at all.

Silty soil is quite similar to sandy soil and can be quite difficult to improve. It retains water better than sand and is often quite fertile but in dry conditions the surface can dry out very easily. This is because the particles of soil are so fine that they can glue together; plants that are not established, such as seedlings, cannot survive this.

Loam

Loam is the gardener's ideal soil. It has good structure and plenty of organic matter and so holds nutrients and water well and is reasonably easy to work. This means it can support a wide range of plants and it will usually host a good population of helpful creatures in the soil. To keep it in top condition, organic matter can be added, which will feed both the soil and the worms.

ACID OR ALKALINE?

On top of this, the soil is going to be either slightly alkaline or slightly acidic, which is measured on a pH scale. The type of soil will indicate to some degree whether it is alkaline or acid. For example, chalk is alkaline, so soil containing a lot of chalk is likely to be alkaline. A peaty, boggy soil would be very acidic, so clay soils (which, like bogs, do not have such good drainage) tend to be acidic.

*The Japanese maple (*Acer palmatum*) has beautiful spring and autumn colour but will only thrive in ericaceous (acid) soil.*

The reason for finding out the soil's pH is that some plants thrive in acidic soils and fail in alkaline soils and vice versa. So if a plant fails to grow healthily, it may simply be a case of having put the wrong plant in the wrong place. This is an important part of understanding how to help plants flourish and why some fail.

It is possible, to a limited degree, to change the soil's pH. For example, adding lime to acidic soil will temporarily help to tip the balance towards a more neutral soil, as you are adding an alkali substance to an acid one. It is far, far easier to learn to love whatever type of soil you have, learn which plants like and loathe those conditions and plant accordingly. Rather than fighting with your soil, it is better to work with it. If you have a favourite plant that fits into the wrong soil type for your soil, then it will often fare better if it is put in a pot with the right compost. For example, blueberries, which require ericaceous soil, can be planted into pots with this soil; this can be bought as bags of compost, and the plants should then be watered only with rainwater.

You can use a special tester to find out the pH of the soil, but the easiest way to find out is to look around at your neighbours' gardens and see what grows well and then find out what conditions the plants that are thriving enjoy; for example, a superb flush of rhododendrons indicates that the soil is acidic.

WHICH PLANT WHERE?

Probably the best indicator of what will succeed in your soil is to look at plants that grow wild in similar conditions to your garden and then see if there are garden cultivars (or the natives themselves) available of the same plant. For example, Field Scabious (*Knautia arvensis*), thrives naturally on chalky meadow soil. This and many cultivars similar to it will therefore thrive in a garden whose soil is alkaline.

Chalky soils, which are generally alkaline, love plants such as Clematis, which make fabulous climbing plants and can provide good cover for birds. The lovely old-fashioned pinks (*Dianthus* spp.) also prefer a chalky soil. Trees also vary in what they

prefer and so it is very important to check when purchasing a tree if it has a soil preference. Lilac (*Syringa vulgaris*) for example, also flourishes growing on alkali soil. If your soil is quite poor, before enriching it with compost, it might be a good idea to try growing a wildflower meadow, which can thrive in poor soil.

Clay soils are better for some moisture-loving plants. If you have ever witnessed the beauty of a heath in full flower, this is a fine example of a plant that thrives in very acidic soil. Heathers are called *Erica carnea* in Latin, and grow in ericaceous soil (which means heath-like, and therefore acid, soil) so you can deduce that heathers and other members of the Ericaceae family, such as *Pieris* spp., will do well if your soil is acid. Trees that mainly dislike chalk, such as most of the ornamental maples (*Acer*

Lilacs prefer to be planted in soil which is alkaline, so chalky limestone soils will suit them.

spp.) provide particularly good autumn colour on acidic soils and most magnolias and shrubs such as camellias and rhododendrons cannot tolerate chalk.

Sandy soils are frequently acidic but because of their free draining habit, they suit drought-tolerant plants that come from hot, dry places. So plants that grow on or near beaches in the wild indicate good plants for sandy soil. For example, the Sea Holly plant (*Eryngium maritimum*) is so named because it grows through very sandy soil on beaches. If you think of those lovely Mediterranean beaches where conifers such as Stone Pines offer a scented shade around sandy bays, this indicates that once established, they are quite drought tolerant and therefore suitable for the sandy soil gardener.

If you are lucky enough to have a good loam soil already, then it should support a range of plants but is particularly useful for growing crops such as vegetables, which take a lot of nutrients from the soil.

Sea hollies and related Eryngium spp. *will grow well in sandy, free draining soil.*

MAKING COMPOST

You may start out life as a gardener finding compost a rather revolting thing – a mass of decaying matter, mouldy old food, grass clippings and goodness knows what living in a heap, amongst your used teabags. However, in time you will learn to love your compost and see it as the most delectable material you can make in your garden, providing a sumptuous feast for your plants.

There are three good reasons for composting: it is the best, most natural substance you can add to your garden; it costs nothing; and it is great for the environment. Wildlife is helped not just by keeping the creatures in the compost heap busy, but it also means you are less likely to buy compost, which would involve transport and packaging, so your composting reduces your impact on the environment in a wider way.

Good compost is composed of a combination of two main ingredients: carbon and nitrogen. Grass cuttings, dead flowers and kitchen waste are high in nitrogen. Chopped-up woody materials, paper and cardboard add carbon. The ratio of green to woody waste should be about one-third green to two-thirds woody.

Compost needs to be moist, but not too wet; to test this, you can squeeze the compost. It should form a ball if it contains the right amount of moisture but shouldn't have water dripping out. If

Composting means that any kitchen waste can be recycled rather than put in the dustbin.

it is too dry, add water or more green materials and if it is too wet, add more dry materials such as paper and card to soak up the excess moisture.

Just as we have got used to recycling general household waste, keep a small container in the kitchen and you will soon get into the habit of putting suitable scraps into it to recycle your kitchen waste. There are now several types of kitchen caddy available to buy, or you can use anything as a container, providing it has a tight-fitting lid.

The compost needs air to break down, so if you have an open compost heap, try to turn it from time to time, taking care that there is no wildlife resident in it at the time (such as hedgehogs). Otherwise, adding a layer of paper or card scrunched up will help. However, if you get it all horribly wrong, the materials will still break down eventually, even without enough air. The final result might be a bit gloopy, but it is still good stuff.

Composting tends to work best if you add quite a lot of material at once, in thin layers of woody and then green waste. To supercharge the compost, a handful of young nettles will act as a natural accelerator (or see the recipe on page 22 for making

WHAT TO COMPOST
Grass clippings
Vegetable peelings and fruit
Twigs and woody material cut into small pieces
Weeds
Hedge clippings
Fallen leaves
Annual and bedding plants
Shredded paper and cardboard
Tea bags and coffee grounds
Straw

WHAT NOT TO COMPOST
Meat, fish or bones
Dairy products or fats
Cooked food
Coal ash
Cat or dog litter
Perennial weeds, or weeds in seed
Diseased material
Woody material thicker than a pencil's width

Spent flower heads and other green waste collected while gardening makes good material for composting.

a liquid feed that can also be watered on to the compost).

Don't expect a huge pile of compost in seconds; composting takes time to produce but the good thing is that it will tick away, slowly turning into a rich, dark matter, even if you ignore it for most of the time. Depending on what you are composting, the position and the type of bin used, composting usually takes a minimum of eight months to break down and most people leave it for a year. The compost is ready when it has turned into a fine, darkish soil and has a sweetish, earthy smell.

Most local authorities have a green waste scheme, which can be used to dispose of perennial weeds, wood and diseased material. Their compost will be heated to higher temperatures, destroying the plants completely, before being recycled as soil conditioner.

Location, location, location

To get started with composting, you first need to decide where to put a compost bin in the garden. The sunnier the spot, the faster the material in it will decompose. The microbes that digest the material ideally like a temperature above 70°C in the compost and they themselves heat it up as they work. This is why if you go past a farmer's yard where manure is being composted, it can actually be steaming with heat.

However, the reality is that most people want the sunny spots for themselves and their prize plants, so the poor old compost gets assigned to a dank corner, where it may take longer to decompose. It is not normally one of the garden's prettiest features, so this is understandable. Remember, though, if you are using the compost for kitchen waste that

On an allotment or in a corner of the garden, it is easy to create a home-made compost bin. Here, a combination of builder's wooden pallets and an innovative use of an old bedstead create a good open bin.

you want it to be near a path that won't be slippery in wet weather and not too far away from the house.

The bottom end of a compost heap should be placed on open earth that has been lightly raked over. This is so that the worms, beetles, centipedes and other insects can find their way up into the bin to help break down the organic matter. It also allows drainage if the heap gets too wet. You might consider placing the bin in a place where you want to enrich the soil for planting up the following year, if you have the type of bin that is easily moved.

Types of compost bin

A huge range of different types of compost bin is available, from enormous plastic objects to the pretty but pricey wooden beehive-style composters.

The very simplest of bins can be made out of old wooden pallets, recycled from a builder's merchants or wood recycling project. There are also wooden kits available for this purpose. Wooden bins are usually open, although a lid will be useful if conditions are very wet or dry, as otherwise the

---

HOW TO MAKE AN OPEN COMPOST BIN

You will need:

- four wooden builder's pallets (you can usually get these free)
- some bits of wood to use for stakes
- a good hammer
- some wire

1. Clear the area where you are going to locate the bin, removing any perennial weeds and making sure the ground is level.
2. Stand one pallet up to form the back of the bin. Put a stake through the pallet, one at either corner. Drive the stakes firmly into the ground to a depth of at least 25cm.

3. Put the other two pallets at right angles to the first one, making sure they are right up against the

back pallet. Drive stakes into each corner of these pallets.

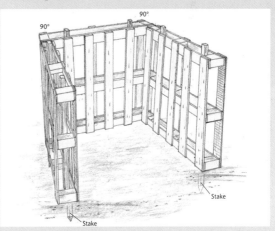

4. Wire the last pallet to the front, to make a gate that can be opened and closed, then wire all the other pallets together to secure them.

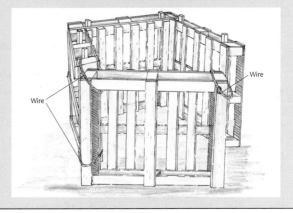

In a small garden, an old barrel with the base cut out can be placed in a sunny spot and used for unobtrusive composting.

compost will require covering with something to protect it.

Open heaps are good if you have the space, in a large garden or on an allotment, but in a small garden one of the manufactured containers may be more suitable. The simplest type of plastic container is a kind of bottomless plastic bin. Most local authorities offer these at a discount to householders to encourage composting. However, using a bin made of recycled wood is less detrimental to the environment in general.

For faster results, there is a kind of composter that is raised off the ground and is called a 'compost tumbler'. They work with a handle that needs to be turned manually each day so that the micro-organisms are constantly being moved around in the soil and the breakdown of material is very efficient. One advantage of this type of composter is that it is therefore rat-proof but it also means that worms and insects do not benefit from it and

animals such as hedgehogs cannot use it as a place to hibernate. This is probably the most expensive type of composter available and it does require constant attention. However, it may suit some types of garden where for some reason a conventional composter is not possible.

Of course, you don't actually have to use a bin at all; it is quite possible to make a compost heap by just piling up materials for composting and covering the area over with something such as old carpet to stop it getting too wet. This probably works best when you have a lot of material all ready to compost in one go. It can be a bit fiddly otherwise, as you will need to cover and uncover the pile if you are adding further waste material.

When the compost is ready, you can just create a new pile, using some of the old compost to start it off, somewhere else. Another idea is to bury waste for compost by digging it into a trench in the garden, which is then covered over with topsoil. This works if you are willing to leave an area undisturbed while the material rots down, but it is not as fast as a compost heap as it does not build up to the same heat.

Wormeries

If you have a small garden or just a patio area and more kitchen than garden waste, it might be worth considering having a wormery. Most wormeries work on a sort of layering system. Food scraps go in at the top, the worms eat this, and the resulting compost and liquid goes down through a series of containers to the bottom levels of the bin. The wormery is closed and unlike an outdoor composter can contain cooked food waste as well as scraps. If the wormery is kept properly, it becomes self-perpetuating, because the worms breed within it.

Wormeries are much smaller than compost bins and can be kept indoors in a cool place or outdoors, depending on the manufacturer's instructions and type of bin chosen. The liquid that is produced is rich and high in nutrients so makes a great plant feed and the compost, although small in quantity, is very good. Wormeries do require dedicated attention: if the liquid is not drained with sufficient frequency, the worms will drown. If the wormery is badly positioned it may be too hot or too cold and if scraps are not added regularly it will dry out and the worms will die.

The most recent idea for breaking down kitchen waste is called a Bokashi bin. This uses an effective micro-organism called Bokashi bran to ferment the material, which can then be put onto compost. It also creates a liquid feed like a wormery. This type of composting allows more types of food to be composted as they are decomposed by the micro-organisms before going into the compost (including items like fish, meat, cheese and eggs, which cannot go on to an outdoor compost heap). Although the composting is anaerobic it is claimed that it does not smell. A disadvantage is that you need to feed it with the special bran, which needs to be purchased, whereas other forms of composting cost nothing. It is, however, rather a good system for places such as restaurants, which have considerable food waste and need to find ways around this.

Getting a compost system going

Some plastic bins have little doors at the bottom from which you are supposed to be able to remove compost, while the material on top is still decomposing. In reality, it is often easier to pick up or tip over the compost bin to get at it. It can be a bit complicated to remove the top layer to get at the compost at the bottom, so ideally it is good to have two bins.

At a certain point you can then leave one bin until the compost is ready and then start on a new bin; then, when this one feels full enough, use the compost from the first bin and start the cycle up again. If you really have a lot of space, a three-compost-bin system is even better: the first bin with compost for use, the second with material being composted and turned, and the third getting new material.

FERTILIZERS

If you are feeding your plants properly with compost and other organic matter, they shouldn't need extra fertilization. If your soil or plants are lacking specific nutrients, consider organic methods to improve them. For example, you can improve the nitrogen levels in your soil by growing beans and digging the plants in after they have been picked. Legumes have nitrogen-fixing nodules in their roots, which will go into the soil.

The use of inorganic fertilizers has long-term consequences: what you hope may be a gain in your garden is actually damaging to the environment as a whole, both in terms of the manufacturing processes and the use of these substances, so the world will benefit if you give these products a miss.

*Comfrey (*Symphytum spp.*) can become quite invasive but it is worth growing a patch to make into liquid fertilizer and the flowers are enjoyed by bees.*

MAKING A NATURAL LIQUID FEED

Liquid fertilizer can be made out of several plants. A patch of nettles in the garden will be useful both for the many insects that need them and also for other plants. Comfrey is another favourite often grown for this purpose. The vigorous Russian Comfrey (*Symphytum* x *uplandicum*) is particularly rich in potash. While both these plants can be rather invasive, using them as a liquid feed will keep their numbers under control and benefit other plants.

To make the fertilizer, chop up young leaves and stems and steep in water in a watertight container. Stir round every few days, until the water turns blackish in colour. The liquid can then be used on plants as a liquid feed, diluted to a measure of 30 parts water to 1 part liquid.

The leaves of both plants, cut before flowering, are rich in nitrogen and can also be used as a compost activator, or as a mulch around hungry plants (but not acid-loving plants) such as potatoes or tomatoes.

MAKING LEAF MOULD

If you have a lot of trees that tend to shed their leaves on the lawn, you may want to make leaf mould. Leaves left on soil will naturally break down and benefit the soil and may also house over-wintering creatures, so there is no need to remove every last leaf in the autumn. However, leaves left on lawns can cause problems and can be turned into leaf mould.

Leaf mould is a humus-rich material that can be added to the soil. It creates the same kind of rich earth that you walk on in woodland. Leaf mould can be sieved for use as a fine potting compost. It can also be used as mulch anywhere in the garden, to improve the structure of the soil. Unlike compost, however, it is not rich in nutrients.

To make leaf mould, simply create a cylindrical container using chicken wire and pile the leaves into it. If you haven't got the space for this, an even simpler method is to gather the leaves in a black bin bag and tuck the bag somewhere out of the way with a heavy stone on top to stop it getting blown about. Add a little bit of water if the leaves are completely dry when you gather them and then just leave it for as long as it takes to turn into organic matter. This is a slow process, which can take up to two years.

If at all possible, just leaving a pile of leaves loose in an undisturbed corner of the garden either as well as or instead of making leaf mould will probably be the most help to wildlife in the garden. Hedgehogs will hibernate in piles of leaves, and insects and other creatures will break them down for you while providing food for hungry birds.

DIGGING AND MULCHING

There was a time when gardeners felt they had to dig over every inch of ground every year. Even worse, some believed that double digging was essential – this means digging to twice the depth of a spade to turn the soil over.

The great thing for the wildlife gardener is that you can spend a lot less time digging and a great deal more actually enjoying your garden. The 'no-dig' movement in gardening is exactly as it is named: the idea is that as living organisms thrive in undisturbed soil, all that you have to do is make sure you add organic mulches to the top of the soil, to keep the structure good.

Digging damages the soil structure, although it does help to aerate it. If you really want to do some digging, then dig out a pond, not your beds and borders.

When you do need to dig

If soil has been very compacted, it may help if you dig it to improve aeration and drainage. Quite often a fork can turn the soil over quite adequately, making the work less heavy than using a spade. To avoid creating compaction on soil, avoid walking over it as much as possible, especially when it is wet and sticky enough to stick to your shoes.

If your garden is overgrown you may also feel you need to dig an area to clear it for planting but again this is not necessarily the case: if you are trying to clear an area of perennial weeds, picking them out manually can be very effective if carried out properly. Annual weeds can be cut off the top of the soil with a hoe. Perennial weeds store their energy in their root systems, so every bit of the roots needs to be removed by hand as you go along. Again, a fork may be more useful than a spade for this, and less heavy. A spade will cut into the soil and slice up perennial weed roots into pieces. Each piece will then become a new plant, making the problem far worse. Forking the soil to find the roots and then picking them out prevents this from happening.

Other methods of ground clearance

In a home garden, there is little excuse these days for using weed killers or any other chemicals, as we now know that that these can be damaging to the environment and enter a food chain where we end up killing the good guys along with the bad guys.

Using a mechanical cultivator is not a good plan for clearing garden land, because it will also chop up perennial weed roots into a thousand new pieces,

While the blackberry is an important food source for wildlife, it may sometimes be necessary to dig up the roots if they are growing in the wrong place.

which will in turn become new weeds. Rotavators can also cause 'panning' of the soil. This means that because the cultivator goes down to the same depth each time it is used, the soil at the bottom gets compacted by this process. Particularly on clay soils, this can create an area that is so hard it creates drainage problems and plant roots cannot break through it either.

A good method of clearing the ground is to cover it with a weed suppressant material. This can be done in two ways. The most thorough method is to hoe off any surface weeds and cover the area, with a very thick layer of mulch – perhaps as much as 30cm. This could be garden compost or other organic matter, depending on what would most benefit the type of soil. The area is then covered with a weed suppressant material.

There are several proprietary types of cover available, but a bit of old builder's tarpaulin or something similar will do. You need to think about whether you want the cover to be waterproof, which means the soil beneath will temporarily dry out, or permeable. If it is waterproof the weeds will also be starved of water but the soil will be hard to work when the cover is removed.

The suppressant needs to be pegged or held down with bricks or stones to keep it in place. After about six months, depending on the season you start in, the underlying growth will have died back and the soil will be ready for planting.

It is also possible to cover the area with weed suppressant on its own and add mulch at a later point. Weed suppressant fabric is very useful and although it looks unattractive this is a small price to pay for the labour saved.

There is a type of flame thrower that can be used to kill off weeds organically. However, this has the disadvantage that it also kills off everything that lives on the weeds, so every insect or any other wildlife that is in its path will be burnt to a crisp too, denuding the area of fauna.

MULCH MAGIC

Mulching is one of the most important ways in which to improve and control the garden. A mulch means any material, organic or otherwise, that is laid on the surface of the soil and is water permeable. It can block out light, suppress weeds, help to warm the soil, retain moisture and improve drainage. In a natural environment, such as a wood, the soil receives a constant supply of decomposing leaves and twigs, which create the dark, earthy surface of the ground and keep the soil conditioned. In order to keep the soil healthy, we therefore have to find ways to recreate mulching.

Inorganic mulches are materials such as manufactured geotextile weed suppressants, or gravel or stones. These are useful in some situations but they do not condition the soil or support insect life. Black plastic sheeting is also sometimes used. This can warm soil up a little but as it is not water permeable the ground beneath it can become dry.

A good layer of mulch spread over the soil will suppress weeds and may add nutrients and also help improve the soil structure.

Old carpet can be used as a weed suppressant but is now being banned from some allotment sites. This is because people may leave it on for so long that weeds start to grow both through it and on it. The carpet starts to decompose and creates a sort of knitted surface that is difficult for someone taking over a plot to clear. Some organic gardeners also argue that carpets may contain chemicals in artificial dyes that will leach into the soil as the carpet breaks down, so that the soil ceases to be organic.

The best mulches are organic materials, which in time are drawn down into the soil. Home-made compost, or well-rotted manure, is a soil conditioner that will add nutrients. If the soil is heavy, a layer of grit will help to open up the soil and improve drainage.

Bark chippings will act well as a weed suppressant and as an attractive ground cover around shrubs and trees but do not add nutrients to the soil. Leaf mould is also good but an ordinary-sized garden is unlikely to produce enough of this to produce a lot of mulch.

Many councils and private individuals will sell different types of mulch, such as bark chippings or composted green waste, for mulching. Farms and stables will often give away manure if you have a place where you can allow it to rot down before use. It is usable when it ceases to smell and has rotted down, which may take up to a year. Spent mushroom compost from mushroom farms is a useful mulch and contains some chalk, so if you wish to balance an acidic soil, this can help.

Cocoa shells can be bought in bags and make a decorative mulch, however these are not advised if you have a dog, as they may unwisely eat it. The shipping involved in bringing these in may also have created rather a large carbon footprint. They may repel slugs, to a degree, but it is expensive when local suppliers can offer suitable materials.

Used straw or hops may not contain many nutrients but can still add structure to the soil. Straw needs to be well rotted in case it contains weed seeds.

A layer of mulch needs to be at least 10cm thick to suppress weeds and ideally perennial weeds should have been removed first, as they will tend to get through it. If it is just required as a soil conditioner, a couple of inches will be better than nothing at all. When adding mulch, always keep it away from touching the base of plants or trees. Plants can suffer from getting 'burnt' because the mulch is still rotting; it is too high in nutrients to be placed on the plants themselves.

Ideally mulch should be applied in the autumn, particularly to heavy soils. Winter frost will help break it down and make the soil easier to work in the spring. Mulch can also be applied any time in the winter, or in the spring to lighter soils, where it gets drawn into the soil faster.

BARE FACTS

The worst thing you can do in your garden is to leave an area of soil completely bare. People often imagine that the presence of areas of bare soil is a sign of a tidy, industrious gardener. Bare soil will be quickly colonized by weeds and it can become eroded. With nothing between it and the sun in the summer, it will also lose moisture rapidly and become baked. It is far better to improve the soil with mulching and then make sure there are plenty of plants acting as a ground cover.

Green manure

One method of treating bare soil is to use what is called 'green manure'. This means growing a crop of a specific plant, which is then dug back into the soil before it flowers, in order to fix nitrogen in the soil and improve the structure as it rots down. Green manure seeds are usually sold alongside ordinary plant seeds. They include clovers and vetches. Rye grass or mustards can also be used, not to fix nitrogen but just to condition the soil.

It is possible to protect soil from erosion and a covering of weeds by planting ground cover. The leaves of Arum Italicum *'Marmoratum', underplanting the Crown imperial (* Fritillaria imperialis) *keeps the ground covered and clear of weeds during spring.*

Phacelia tanecetifolia *is a very attractive plant to grow for bees and can be used as a green manure.*

CHAPTER 3

Creating a balance in the garden

By definition, if you are gardening for wildlife, you will be gardening organically. Ideally, no pesticides, herbicides or fungicides at all should be used in the garden, which is a further step on from organic thinking. Immediately, this begs the question: how can you then control weeds and pests in the garden?

There are two key ways in which to control a garden. The first is to create a balance in the garden, so that for nearly every pest there is a predator and for every weed there are other plants that will prevent it from colonizing the space. The second way to keep the garden as you want it is through knowledge of the weeds and pests themselves.

UNDERSTANDING MINI-BEASTS

Looking at the problems of pests first, the first part of that knowledge is learning to distinguish between insects and other creatures that help and insects that harm plants. This will greatly improve your chances of keeping a healthy garden. It is also helpful to know about their lifecycles, so that you can encourage helpful insects to survive through the seasons. This can be done by creating artificial habitats, to make your garden not just a place to visit but a happy home for many hard-working species.

Recognizing what insects you have doesn't then mean exterminating every aphid that you come across – they will be food for many helpful insects and birds – but identifying different insects and other creatures and what they do to plants will help you keep in touch with what is going on and

in itself can become quite fascinating. So a wildlife gardener's motto should perhaps be 'stop before you squash' and check out if the insect really is harmful.

Some insects may be annoying on one plant but also helpful, so for example earwigs will nibble away at dahlias, which is annoying, but also eat aphids, which is good. It is therefore probably best to protect plants if you spot the signs of damage from a specific insect, rather than attempting to wipe out the population of this insect, which you are unlikely to be able to do anyway.

Understanding more about helpful insects will naturally lead to stopping the use of pesticides. Even organic ones will be harmful to some of the insects that can control difficult pests in the garden, so if you use pesticides, you are wiping out nearly everything. Some pesticides claim to be safe to use

Dahlias can end up being nibbled by earwigs but these insects will also control aphids, so it is best to just try to protect vulnerable plants rather than destroying them.

A garden which is good for wildlife will have a diverse variety of plants, shrubs and trees.

around bees, but these are not the only insects that need protecting. Added to which, a sterile, pest-free environment means there will be no insect food in your garden to attract birds.

By messing around with one part of the food chain, we are messing around with all of it as the balance of predators and prey gets disturbed. The creatures we actually want to attract will not wish to visit our gardens if there is nothing for them to eat and no place for them to breed or shelter.

Knowledge also means putting the right plants into the right environment, so that they will naturally be healthy and less likely to be attacked by pests and diseases. A plant that is likely to suffer from mould is not ideal for a moist, humid spot, for example. The use of fungicides is also often damaging to the environment.

BIODIVERSITY

On farms and in domestic vegetable gardens and allotments, many people have developed mono-cultures. This means growing just one single plant in an area, so in farming, a field of one crop, or an orchard garden with just apples. On a commercial level, this makes cropping much easier but creates two problems. Firstly, the soil becomes deprived of the mixture of nutrients that is needed to keep the plants healthy, because each specific plant takes specific nutrients from the soil. This means that artificial fertilizers are required to keep the plants growing well, which often means adding chemicals.

The lack of diversity also means that the crops suffer a build-up of pests and diseases. Because there are no other plants growing in the area, other insects, which might be predatory on the pests, cannot sustain themselves. No alternative is then left but to spray chemicals onto the pests, to prevent the crop being ruined. So the result of a mono-culture means a deathly environment with no place for wildlife.

In our gardens or allotments, we may also have monocultures, for example, a close-cropped lawn, where no weeds are allowed, or just rows and rows of the same vegetable growing. When it comes to growing something such as vegetables or fruit, rows may be the easiest style in terms of access and to

Learning to recognize helpful insects, such as the hoverfly, makes a good start in creating balance in a wildlife garden.

*The poached-egg plant (*Limnanthes douglasii*) will attract beneficial insects to a specific area of the garden.*

adding colour and form to otherwise dull areas where vegetables or fruit may be grown. It can also be used where there is a monoculture such as a rose bed, to help protect this prized plant from aphids.

By understanding as much as we can about pests and diseases, we can also break the cycle that keeps some of them going. This may be especially helpful where plants are being grown as crops, in a vegetable patch. Pests and diseases may require a host plant throughout the year to keep going. For example, whitefly will overwinter on winter brassicas such as Brussels sprouts. Once the harvest has been taken from these plants, it is a good idea to dig up and dispose of the plants completely. That way, it isn't possible for the whitefly to survive and their life cycle is broken.

When growing vegetables in the garden or on an allotment it is always a good idea to remember the old idea of rotation. This idea is as old as the hills and prevents a build-up of pathogens in the soil. With vegetables, this follows a three-year pattern created by putting the crops into three main categories: brassicas, roots and legumes. So for example, cabbages are brassicas, carrots are root vegetables and beans are legumes. Each year, the position where these crops are planted is rotated. For instance, a broad bean will not be planted in the same place that had peas (also in the legume family) growing the previous year.

Similarly, if onions are always planted in the same place, then if they get onion rot, this will happen

weed around the crops to prevent competition from other plants but it is far better to intersperse crops with other plants that will attract predatory insects that will do the pest controlling for us.

This is one of the principles of companion planting, which means for every plant you put in that will need protection, you create a companion for it, which is a plant that in one of several ways helps the plant you want to grow. In its simplest form, this may mean growing flowers amongst vegetables. Companion planting looks wonderful,

Understanding the life cycle of the cabbage white butterfly whose caterpillars are show here, makes controlling them much easier.

year after year to the onions if they continue to be planted in the same place, because the disease will remain in the soil. If onions are not planted there for some years after onion rot has occurred and the soil is used for other purposes, the earth has a chance to recover and the pathogens will slowly die away if they do not have a host plant in the Allium family.

The idea of rotating crops around a plot is extremely good but in a garden it may also be a good idea to move a crop plot to a different area occasionally, so that the same plot is not always continuously used for crops, or to plant a few crops amongst ornamentals.

In the ornamental garden, fruit trees and roses are also examples of plants that don't do well if they are replaced with more of the same. The soil builds up disorders because a specific plant will always remove the same nutrients and denude the soil, creating ideal conditions for disease. In the case of roses, the soil develops a well-known disorder that creates what is called 'rose sickness', so it is always good to avoid replanting where a similar plant has already been growing.

A rose garden can look very effective but continually replanting roses in the same spot can create a build up of disease in the soil.

FRIENDS AND ENEMIES

As gardeners we very quickly tend to categorize the creatures we encounter in our gardens as 'good' and 'bad'. Slugs and snails drive us up the wall, munching their way through our plants, yet the hedgehog or slow-worm needs them to survive. If we start to think of the garden as some sort of battleground, it ceases to be a relaxing and enjoyable place to be. So we need to start to relax our attitude to creatures we consider to be the baddies and accept that they are just part of the natural process of wildlife gardening, just trying to earn an honest living eating plants.

Slugs and snails

In a wildlife garden, slug pellets should ideally be avoided completely, even if they are described as 'friendly' or organic. They don't just poison slugs but get into the food chain of the animals that eat slugs and can affect birds, frogs and hedgehogs and pets. Killing slugs and snails can become an unhappy habit, using beer traps, 'safe' slug pellets or going out at night with a torch and picking them off plants.

The usefulness of killing slugs and snails is arguable in that as with many creatures, if a vacuum is created, more will come into the area to enjoy the fresh green plants. Unloved as they are, slugs and snails are only doing what comes naturally to them and in turn provide food for other animals. Perhaps it is time we learned, perhaps not to hug a slug, but at least to cease to view them as something that must always be exterminated.

Protecting young plants

Protecting plants rather than attacking slugs and snails is perhaps a more positive and defensive line to take. Plants most at risk of being polished off completely are seedlings and very young plants. The longer they can be kept in a protected environment before they have to face the big wide world the better; the mature leaves of strong, healthy plants are much less attractive to the slug. Hardening off plants is also important. This means putting them out in the daytime and taking them in at night or when it is very wet or cold, so that they harden up ready for planting out.

If you want to sow seeds directly into the ground, then seedlings may need protecting as they come up. Plastic cloches, bought, or made out of upturned

Prevention is always better than cure; putting a collar around this young cabbage prevents the cabbage root fly from laying its eggs around the roots of the plant and eventually destroying it.

plastic bottles, offer a warm environment that offers some protection from invertebrates and can be removed when the plants are more established. They also protect plants against wind and frost when they are young and vulnerable and can be useful to prevent pigeons pecking at young plants, particularly in the winter.

For food plants, collars can be made or bought to put around the base of vegetables that are liable to have their roots damaged by, for example, cabbage root fly. These work by preventing the flies from laying their eggs close enough to the plant roots for any damage to be done to the crops.

If you are not willing to share fruit crops with the birds, or they are damaging buds and plants, another method of protection is netting plants. Serious fruit-growers may wish to create a permanent fruit cage and vegetables can be protected within this too; however, netting may also be used temporarily to protect a harvest. Netting can be harmful to birds, as they can get caught in it; even with a fruit cage it is important to check regularly that no birds have managed to get in and cannot escape.

The timing of some plantings may also influence whether or not the plant is liable to get overcome by a specific pest. Peas that are sown very early, for example, either in later winter or early spring, will flower too early for the pea moth to lay its eggs in their flowers, because they only do this in the summer.

An insurance policy is also a good idea; rather than sowing all your seeds out in one go, or planting them all out together, keep some back, or sow some inside and then if they do get eaten, you haven't lost everything and you know that the planting spot you chose may be troublesome for seedlings. Sometimes just moving plants to another part of the garden can decrease their risk of getting eaten before they have had a chance to grow up.

Slugs and snails like moist conditions and don't like travelling over sharp material. Therefore putting grit or sharp sand around popular plants is helpful, or a collar of smashed up eggshells, seashells or coarse sandpaper. On pots, slugs and snails are supposed to be averse to copper as it carries a tiny electric charge, so a copper ring can be put around a pot or precious plant. It is also possible to make

Snails can be a nuisance in the garden but also provide food for wildlife. Learning which plants are most at risk helps to keep the garden growing.

about the damage caused by slugs and snails, it might be worth considering replacing some of the plants that are known to attract slugs and snails with other plants that are known to be more slug resistant. Hostas, for example, are often grown in the sort of damp, shady conditions beloved by slugs and get completely demolished. They are not a native plant and so have no resistance to slugs. Delphiniums also attract slugs; some cottage gardeners will ruin an otherwise organic and chemical-free garden in order to grow these by littering the surrounding ground with slug pellets. Slugs and snails will travel far and wide to get to the plants, and then hang out in your garden eating anything else that is around.

Far better to grow the hoodie of the flower world, *Aconitum napellus*, as an alternative. This has tall, beautifully divided leaves like a Delphinium and gorgeous racemes of indigo-blue flowers in mid-summer, which appear slightly hooded, hence its common name, Monkshood. It will grow in quite shady conditions but doesn't attract the attention of our slimy friends.

One of the reasons slugs can chomp their way through our plants so successfully is that so many plants we wish to grow in our garden are not native species and are not adapted to the conditions of our country and our slugs. They put on soft growth that is irresistible to a passing slug or snail, whereas native plants have more defences with tougher leaves that are less attractive to the mollusc mob.

GETTING TO KNOW THE WEEDS

Just as we need to get to know our plants in order to give them the best life in a wildlife garden, we also need to get to know the weeds. The sooner we can identify what they are when they come up, the better. It is often said that a weed is just a plant growing in the wrong place. However, many weeds will grow not just in the wrong place, but all over the place.

When introducing a new plant to a garden, which may have been given to you or come from an unknown source, always check the soil it is planted in carefully for weed roots or seeds. Sometimes weeds such as Hedge bindweed (*Calystegia sepium*),

a spray of one bulb of crushed garlic boiled in a pint of water and strained. Sprayed on to the leaves of plants, this appears to have some benefit in deterring slugs and snails, which don't like the smell. However, it may also deter beneficial insects and of course it washes off in rain.

Some plants just have the misfortune to be slug and snail manna. Rather than getting into a lather

Plants such as nettles that we see as weeds are a vital resource in the life cycle of some butterflies.

which can be annoying, can be innocently introduced into your garden wrapped around the roots of a new plant.

Weeds are really very successful plants and one has to admire their ability to survive. They start to become a problem for the gardener when they compete with plants that you want to grow and take up the nutrients those plants need from the soil. Eventually, they will overshadow the plant, depriving it of light. Some also shelter pests and diseases, which then get transferred to other plants.

The second way in which we can conquer problem weeds, having first identified them, is to get to know their life cycles and methods of reproduction. There are many different ways in which weeds can arrive and spread in the garden. As every child who has played with a dandelion clock will know, some weed seeds will be dispersed by wind and some can even be brought in on the soles of our shoes.

Methods of weeding are simple to learn. Knowing what to weed can be a little harder. The most important thing to understand, to keep weeds under control without chemicals, is to recognize whether you are dealing with an annual or perennial weed.

As with garden plants, weeds can be divided into annuals, biennials and perennials. (There are also a few plants called ephemerals, which are able to reproduce more than once in a year.) Annuals grow, flower, set seed and die within one year. Biennials put on leafy growth in the first year, flower and set seed in the second year and then die. Perennials often have fleshy roots that enable them to die back in the winter and return every year. Other types of perennials may have thick rosettes of leaves, so that a common lawn weed such as Plantain (*Plantago* spp.) starts to smother surrounding grass.

Annual and biennial weeds are fairly easy to control, once they are spotted. They tend to have shallow roots, so if hand weeding or a hoe is used to pull them off the soil, they will die quickly. In fact, if the weather is dry they can even be left to die on top of the soil. The art of getting rid of unwanted annuals and biennials is to make sure you have disposed of them before they set seed, otherwise a whole new generation will turn up the following year. Again, if they are not particularly invasive, some seed heads might be good for birds, so only pull them up if you think you need to.

Perennial weeds are more difficult to tackle. It is important not to chop up the roots, which is often done by people vigorously digging or rotavating over soil. Each bit of root just becomes another weed on its own, so you can make a small problem much larger. So forking out the plants individually is the best idea. Plants like dandelions (*Taraxacum vulgaris*) and dock (*Rumex* spp.) can build up huge tap roots.

Hedge bindweed (Calystegia sepium) *is a perennial weed which can be quite deep rooted. It can eventually be controlled if it is continually removed below the soil level.*

Hedge and field bindweeds (*Calystegia sepium* and *Convolvulus arvensis*) and Horsetail (*Equisetum* spp.) are all examples of weeds that have spreading, deep roots that creep along underground. They can be hard to control. Sometimes it is worth putting down light-excluding fabric for a few seasons until it dies, but one must not be too hasty in removing it.

Couch Grass (*Elymus repens*), Ground Elder (*Aegopodium podagraria*) and nettles (*Urtica dioica*) have shallow roots, but they spread outwards and each bit of rhizome or root will create another plant. Once again, digging, which will chop up the roots

into many pieces, is not a good idea. Forking out the roots is the best idea but it may take several attempts to clear it away completely as just one small piece will start a new weed. If the area is very matted, it may be worth covering with light-excluding fabric for a few seasons.

Some weeds put out runners (in the way that strawberries do), which can form plantlets further along the ground, for example, the Creeping Buttercup (*Ranunculus repens*), which can be forked up. Weeds with bulbils will be spread by cultivation and two of these, Pink Oxalis (*Oxalis articulata*) and Lesser Celandine (*Ranunculus ficaria*), require hand digging to get out all the tiny bulbils, or using light-excluding material for several seasons, as the bulbs will survive for some time without light. However, as they are both very attractive plants, it may be

Ground elder (Aegopodium podagraria) *has roots that spread outwards to create many new plants in the area.*

worth just trying to keep them in check rather than hoping to remove them totally.

Many of these weeds also flower and set seed, so tackling weeds early in the year is essential to prevent flowering. They are also good at out-competing garden plants because many of them flower before anything else gets going, so they grab a bigger share of space. One has to admire the ingenuity of nature in creating so many ways for weeds to sneak past even the most diligent gardener.

Weeds for wildlife

Gardening for wildlife does not mean you have to tolerate all weeds, but some insects use weeds as part of their life cycle. They also provide food for many birds. Something like Teasel (*Dipsacus fullonum*), which can be an invasive weed, is also an important food source for birds in the winter and provides a shelter for some overwintering insects.

Not all weeds are hugely invasive and there is no harm in changing your outlook on tolerating the less invasive ones. They may not have been invited to the party, but some of them can turn out to be quite acceptable guests.

Many weeds are particularly good for encouraging wildlife and can also make attractive ground cover, which may prevent other more invasive plants taking over. At the base of hedging, Red Dead Nettle (*Lamium purpureum*) and Ground Ivy (*Glechoma hederacea*) both make attractive ground cover and have pretty flowers that bees will love. In the lawn, clovers (*Trifolium* spp.) are well worth tolerating for the same reason.

Some native plants that we may think of as weeds will often be included in a native wildflower seed mixture, such as Field Poppies (*Papaver rhoeas*). A pretty May mist of Cow Parsley (*Anthriscus sylvestris*) can look great in a long meadow and will attract the beneficial hoverfly insect into the garden. Small weeds such as Fumitory (*Fumaria spp.*) and Wild Pansy (*Viola tricolor*) tend to turn up in ground that has been turned over. They are delightful and not particularly invasive, so can be allowed a stay of execution in a wildlife garden. Fumitory can easily be pulled up if it gets too ambitious.

Quite a lot of weeds have at one time or another been valued as food plants or for their herbal uses.

*A plant such as Common fumitory (*Fumaria officinalis*) is so attractive that it might be worth considering it to be rather an over-enthusiastic flower, rather than a weed.*

Wild Garlic Mustard (*Alliaria petiolata*) can be added to salads and young nettles are renowned for making a fantastic spring soup. Even some of the tiny annuals such as Chickweed (*Stellaria media*) can be gathered for a spring salad but of course correct identification is vital when picking wild plants that appear in the garden.

Dandelion root, roasted, makes an acceptable drink and young leaves can be forced to add bitterness to salads. Nettles are important plants for a number of creatures including butterflies and along with Comfrey, make excellent compost and liquid fertilizer for the better-bred plants in the garden.

As will be discussed later in the context of wildflower meadows, lawns do not have to be a monoculture of grass: many weeds, such as daisies, are attractive, add to the character of a lawn and are very useful plants for wildlife.

CHAPTER 4

Birds in the garden

The presence of birds in a garden quickly becomes a huge source of entertainment, whether we are watching them from indoors or out. Birds also help us to remember to stop sometimes and be still in the garden, as it is only then that we can really watch them closely.

The population of birds that frequent gardens is plummeting rapidly. There are many ways in which every gardener can try to reverse this trend. The first thing to consider is how to grow food sources for birds. Garden birds can be identified in terms of the food they eat as omnivores, insect eaters, seed eaters and fruit eaters.

INSECT EATERS

Apart from the birds that catch insects on the wing, such as swifts, swallows and house martins, many birds catch insects while they are feeding on garden plants. Birds such as goldcrests, chiffchaffs and wrens feed in this way. Insect-feeding birds are unlikely to feed at a bird table, as the food doesn't meet their needs. Once you become aware of these birds, annoying insects such as aphids suddenly cease to feel like a pest and you start to view them as a vital food supply for the birds. Some birds, including many songbirds, use insects as a food source just for when they are feeding their young.

Killing insects in the garden effectively means killing birds. Even the apparently 'safe' pesticides may create a build-up of poisons in insects, which can then accumulate in the bodies of insect-eating

The robin is a favourite bird and will happily hover around the working gardener, hoping for a worm.

birds. The idea that gardening means eliminating an entire food source for birds, in order to have blemish-free plants, is a little out of date. Now we know the effects of pesticides anyone who wishes to garden responsibly should reconsider their use in the garden.

Sadly, people are most inclined to use pesticides at the start of the growing season when they spot the first insects appearing, which coincides with the time when many birds desperately need the insects to feed their young. It also means that those insects that are natural predators on insects we consider pests, will also be unable to carry out their duties, as they will move on to other gardens in search of food sources.

Insect-eating birds will anyway struggle to find enough food in urban gardens due to the lack of suitable plants to attract the insects. Traffic pollution in densely populated areas may also limit the availability of insects as toxins from this may build up and affect the survival of some insects.

A wildflower area such as a mini-meadow will attract a good range of insects for the birds and a garden pond will have midges or mosquitoes to which the flycatchers, swifts and swallows will be attracted.

SEED EATERS

The tree sparrow, greenfinch, crossbill, brambling and goldfinch are all entirely reliant on seeds for their diet. This can make their lives very difficult, as they have been hit hard by changes in agricultural farming methods. Most seeds ripen in the summer or autumn, so winter and spring can be hard times for the seed eaters. Seed-eating birds

PLANTS FOR INSECT EATERS

*On this allotment, a combination of Golden rod (*Solidago spp.) *Teasel (*Dipsacus fullonum) *and Ox-eye daisies (*Chrysanthemum leucanthemum) *attract insects which provide plenty of food for birds.*

Bird Cherry (*Prunus padus*)
Fern-leaved Yarrow (*Achillea filipendula*)
Golden Rod (*Solidago virgaurea*)
Honesty (*Lunaria annua*)
Lavender (*Lavandula angustifolia*)
Lemon Balm (*Melissa officinalis*)

PLANTS FOR SEED EATERS

*The milk thistle (*Silybum marianum) *is easily grown and provides seeds which are edible by birds. Humans also use the plant as a herb for liver complaints.*

Amaranth (*Amaranthus caudatus*)
Milk Thistle (*Silybum marianum*)
Millet (*Panicum miliaceum*)
Red Clover (*Trifolium pratense*)
Sunflower (*Helianthus annuus*)
Teasel (*Dipsacus fullonum*)

It is really important to leave seed heads on plants during the autumn and winter as these are a valuable food source for seed-eating birds.

seriously reconsider whether to tolerate this invasive weed, as the sudden flickers of colour that these birds bring into the garden may finally persuade the hardest-hearted of gardeners to stop using weed killer on the lawn.

Seed eaters can be of service to the gardener, too. They perform a useful garden function in the winter, as they may forage for seeds in the soil, potentially reducing the return of annual weeds the following season.

FRUIT-EATING BIRDS AND OMNIVORES

The garden warbler and the redwing eat only fruit; blackcaps, mistle thrushes and fieldfares have a fruit diet but supplement it with insects, or seeds. The omnivores eat fruit when it is around and some are identifiable by having longish beaks. This includes blackbirds, collared doves and robins. These birds have to turn to fruit in the winter when the ground is frozen and it is not possible for them to forage for food such as worms, grubs or seeds.

Birds are most attracted to red or orange-coloured berries and will eat these in preference to other colours, such as white or yellow. So if you want to keep a display of berries for longer through

will readily take food from a bird table to help them through these times, although it may take a while for them to get used to a new seed type offered to them.

Dunnocks, siskins, linnets, great tits, nuthatches and reed buntings are able to vary their diet with insects; they can eat these during spring and summer when seeds are in short supply and their presence may help control insects for the gardener. Bullfinches are seed eaters, but unfortunately they also sometimes have a penchant for pecking at fruit buds, which can make them rather less popular visitors with fruit growers.

If you find you have a lawn full of dandelions, many insects will feed on the flowers and the seeds are a very good food for small seed-eating birds. Watching a couple of goldfinches demolishing dandelion clocks with such relish can make you

The blackbird will feed on earthworms and insects but as it originally lived in woodlands and hedges, it also has a taste for fruit and berries.

the winter, choose plants with the latter colours. Otherwise, enjoy the spectacle of the birds gorging themselves on the red berries as they prepare for the hard times ahead.

Even the smallest of gardens can afford to include a small shrub or tree with suitable berries to feed birds and whether or not you additionally feed birds, providing them with a natural source of food that they can expect annually is the best way to garden for wildlife.

While some fruits such as those of the Guelder rose are dispatched quickly by birds and the remainder rot if not taken, Holly and Cotoneaster berries will remain edible for a longer period and are therefore a good choice for providing a winter food source for birds. Ideally, having plants that fruit at different times will give the birds their best chance of survival.

It is fairly easy to provide food for the fruit eaters, providing we are willing to share our own harvest. Leaving a few apples or pears or dried fruit lying around will allow ground feeders such as blackbirds to peck away to their heart's content and starlings will enjoy any fruit left around.

Fruit such as strawberry plants can be important as an early source of fruit. If you are not willing to share your prize fruits, growing wild (or Alpine) strawberries (*Fragaria vesca*) that look attractive but are a bit small and fiddly for human tastes, will keep the birds happy.

Many birds that eat fruit have a special adaptation: their digestive tract lengthens in winter, so that they can take fruit when there are few available insects. Unfortunately the right food is not always available at the right time, so despite the name of omnivore, they are sometimes hard pressed to find appropriate food.

Some of the larger birds will also eat smaller birds or chicks, which gives these birds a better survival rate. Members of the crow family are the main culprits, such as magpies, jays and jackdaws. Seagulls have also adapted by scavenging, although despite appearing ubiquitous in some areas, the number of herring gulls is actually dwindling. Of course the thrush is much loved by the gardener, as it will eat snails, by first smashing their shells against a rock or hard surface.

*Wild or alpine strawberries (*Fragaria vesca *and* F. moschata*) look pretty growing amongst marjoram (*Oreganum spp.*) and provide an early source of food to fruit-eating birds.*

PLANTS FOR FRUIT EATERS

The attractive flowers of a cultivar of elderberry,
Sambucus nigra *'Black Lace' are followed by clusters
of black berries in the autumn on which birds gorge
themselves.*

Elderberry (*Sambucus nigra*)
Herringbone Cotoneaster (*Cotoneaster horizontalis*)
Holly (*Ilex aquifolium*)
Honeysuckle (*Lonicera periclymenum*)
Rowan (*Sorbus aucuparia*)
Guelder Rose (*Viburnum opulus*)

FEEDING BIRDS

The best thing you can do for birds is to grow plants
that provide food for them and a good wildlife
garden should go some way to doing this. However,
as garden birds are in such decline, most wildlife
organizations would agree that supplementary
feeding of birds is important because of their
declining numbers.

The best way to keep the birds in a good
condition is to feed them sources of food that they
would naturally eat. For the seed eaters this might
include black sunflower seed hearts, niger seed
(loved by goldfinches) and millet seed. Species of
birds are adapted in the wild to different types
of food sources and have different types of beaks
accordingly. The small bill of the siskin, for example,
can extract seeds from alder, birch or pine cones.

Seed feeders need and prefer seeds that are high
in oil. Wisely, they are usually wary of food sources
that are not familiar to them; they may avoid them
initially, so allow them time to adapt. There are
migratory seed feeders, such as bramblings, siskins
and many finches, so sometimes the birds are short-
term visitors to the garden. Resident species also
move around, between areas where they breed and
foraging areas, in the winter.

Many mixes can be bought which also contain
nut granules, husk-free oats, maize and dried

*Sometimes the guests at bird feeders are not the ones you
expect, as this herring gull demonstrates.*

fruits. Take care that peanuts are fresh and from a reliable supplier, as they can contain aflatoxin, which can poison birds. Salted peanuts, or any dry, hard or salty foods should be avoided. It may be best to avoid large chunks of food such as bread, or loose peanuts during the nesting season, as there is considered to be a possibility that chicks could choke if they were fed by the parent in large chunks.

Fat balls or bars are a great winter supplement for many birds. They should be removed from the plastic meshing they often come in and put into a proper feeding container, to prevent small birds getting their feet caught in the mesh. It is really important not to stop feeding birds when the spring arrives. This is actually the time of year when food is at its most limited, as insects have not yet appeared and seeds are not set. Added to which, the birds are starting to breed and need food to keep them going, while they search for live food for the chicks. Continuing to feed during the summer may encourage fledglings to treat your garden as base camp, particularly during the winter.

Worms such as waxworms or mealworms are ideal for nesting birds, as these can be fed directly to the young and the protein will help them build up their wing muscles. Robins, as many gardeners will know, will learn to hang around a gardener turning over the soil, in the hope a few worms will be left lying around for them. They can also be fed with mealworms (either live or dried) and soon learn to take them from your hand. It is best to feed robins away from other birds if possible; as sweet as we find them, they can be rather aggressive and territorial.

Of human food, many ordinary household scraps can be placed on the bird table but take care not to leave food to go mouldy. Unsalted cooked rice, breadcrumbs, cake crumbs, grated cheese and even pet foods can be offered. Cooked foods such as vegetables, particularly potatoes, can also be put out in moderation. Hanging up a half coconut is a great way to watch birds feed. Raw oats are good, but not cooked porridge oats, because the gluten could possibly glue up their beaks.

It is probably best if possible to feed birds in the morning, so that the food is gone by the evening and doesn't attract rats. However, remember some birds are ground feeders, such as blackbirds, so they do need food to be left at ground level.

Bird tables and feeders

There are many attractive styles of bird feeders and tables but the most important factors in the long run are that they are stable and can be easily cleaned. Make sure the table has a rim to keep the food on it but also has gaps in the corner so that rainwater can run off the table top easily.

Bird feeders come in a range of shapes and sizes which will attract different types of birds.

If you do not want or have space for a bird table, food can be scattered on the ground, or you can just hang up individual feeders on, for example, a tree. You can even smear fat onto trees or posts. Think carefully about where you position feeders so that they aren't close to an area where a cat can easily stalk the feeding birds.

It is important not to leave food lying around as a build-up of harmful bacteria could poison the birds. Putting food out little and often is the best plan, adding more only as the current supply is ending. Birds can pick up many diseases from each other, especially at feeding stations where they gather densely. It is therefore vital to keep the feeders and tables clean, otherwise you could be doing more harm than good trying to feed them.

First of all, keep a bucket, brushes and gloves somewhere outside especially for cleaning the bird tables and feeders. It soon becomes clear that styles of feeders that are easier to clean are preferable. Clean both feeders and water baths with a special disinfectant for this purpose, or use bleach, diluted down to a solution of 1 part bleach to 20 parts water. After cleaning, rinse very thoroughly and dry completely before putting back. Water baths should be washed regularly as well in the same way.

Always wash your hands after they have been in contact with the feeding stations or baths. In order to stop food and droppings building up too much in one area, move feeders around. Also, allow plenty of space between feeders if you have many different birds, so they are not all competing in one small area.

Birds and water

Whether or not you choose to feed birds, providing water is essential. This is not just during the summer, when drought may make access to water difficult for birds, but also throughout the year and particularly during cold spells in the winter when other sources of water may be frozen.

The water needs to be changed regularly to keep it fresh. Birds require water not just for drinking but to keep their feathers in good condition by bathing in it. A bird bath will be a great source of amusement as birds dip in and out for a wash, but must be kept clean to prevent diseases spreading

amongst them. Birds wash to keep free of dust and parasites; some species such as blackbirds, robins and pigeons are very fond of a bath whereas some hardly bother to bathe at all. Most birds need a gentle slope down into water to get in and out easily, so if you have a wildlife pond, make sure one part of it has a gentle slope into the water, or create one with a variety of stones and pebbles.

If you are specifically providing a bird bath and it is not being used, put a few pebbles in the bottom as it might be that it is too deep for smaller birds to get in and out of. Ideally, it is good to have both a shallow vessel, such as an ornamental bird bath, and a pond for a deeper bird bath. Make sure one lot of drinking water and bath water are put in a clearing, with an escape into high branches close by, so that the birds can both see, and make a dash for it, if a predator turns up. Other birds may prefer a bath low down, very close to cover rather than in a clearing.

Although there are many lovely designs for bird baths, it isn't essential to splash out on one, as they can easily be improvised if you prefer.

You could also consider providing a dust bath for birds such as house sparrows, simply by leaving a dry area of ground bare, for them to preen their feathers in.

PREDATORS

Birds have a variety of natural predators. In the garden, magpies and large birds will raid nests and take eggs, and sparrowhawks will sometimes swoop down and audaciously remove a favourite garden visitor.

Squirrels will sometimes try to take birds' eggs, so make sure nest boxes have a secure lid that they can't open. A slippery bit of drainpipe will protect a bird table, or a cage may protect the area.

Cats in the garden

Cats can cause two problems for wildlife gardeners. Firstly, they are the biggest killer of garden birds. They are responsible for the deaths of millions of birds, every year. Secondly, some gardeners can also get annoyed by cats that use areas of ground as a

Cats are sometimes despised for causing problems in the garden but they are only following their instincts in hunting birds, mice and voles.

toilet. However, cats are only doing what is natural to them, and it is not their fault that we have such a disproportionate number of them in gardens; this is a human decision, not the cats' idea.

Fresh soil with very little on it, such as seedlings, is particularly attractive to them, as is some gravel. If cats are a problem in the garden, it may be worth protecting newly planted areas from them, perhaps using something like netting, or another physical barrier. They may also sharpen their claws on bark to mark their territory so vulnerable young trees may need a tree guard.

Cats are creatures of habit, so if you want to stop an area being used as a toilet, you need first to remove any faeces, so the area doesn't smell. There are a variety of products to discourage cats, which have a scent or taste that they dislike. Some products contain essential oils that can be put down for short-term use. It may be worth considering growing a plant called *Coleus canina* near to favourite plants. The *Coleus* produces a smell disliked by cats when brushed past.

Other repellents involve motion water sprays or ultrasonic sound sensors. The latter may unfortunately be audible to other animals, such as foxes or badgers. Generally, keeping soil moist will make it less appealing, as cats don't really like getting their paws wet. They will also be less likely to bother with densely planted areas, where there is plenty of ground cover. It may also be that a garden that is attractive to wildlife such as foxes ceases to attract cats, which don't like the scent of foxes.

If you have a cat that catches birds (and not all of them do) then it may be worth changing its feeding times, so that it is fed nearer to dawn and dusk. These are the times when the birds are most active in the garden, so keeping the cat distracted might at least cut down on the numbers. Bells on cats' collars are sometimes suggested but it has to be seriously considered whether it is fair to doom a cat to a lifetime of tinnitus. However, many wildlife organizations feel they may be the only answer for some cats.

The positioning of bird feeders is also important. If you have a cat around, don't feed birds in a place that offers a hiding place for Tiddles close by, such as bushes or low trees. There are also various devices that can be used to stop cats and squirrels climbing up bird tables.

For cat lovers there are a couple of other things worth considering in the general scheme of wildlife. Owning one cat is understandable but although many people get more cats 'to keep each other company', there are plenty of cats for company outside anyway. One cat will have a certain impact on a bird population, but the more cats there are concentrated in one area, the more devastating the effect on the birds. A wild cat might have had a range of about 10km^2, per cat. It is therefore worth considering whether to stick to just one cat as a concession to wildlife.

Chicks in nest boxes are particularly vulnerable, so make sure they are fixed somewhere out of reach of little paws. If the box has an opening top, as suggested for cleaning out bird boxes, then make sure there is also a way of securing the top down during the nesting season.

It may also be worthwhile to think about getting a cat neutered. There are thousands of unwanted pet cats and kittens in the country, so getting a cat neutered can help stop the population explosion. Also, it could be argued that if you buy a cat or kitten, you are encouraging people to breed more cats, whereas if you make sure your cat or kitten comes from a rescue centre, you are not contributing to breeding a species of which we already have a surplus.

I think we have to think hard about being responsible about the impact they have on all wildlife. The millions of birds per year that are killed are joined in ranks by countless slow-worms, newts, mice, moths and bats, amongst other creatures.

However, having a wildlife friendly garden may actually help out the wildlife and birds, even if you have a cat. This is because if you have provided plenty of the elements that birds need, for shelter, food and water, they are more likely to visit the garden in numbers. The more of them there are around, the faster the alarm call goes up that there is a cat about and so they all have a better chance to fly off.

HOMES AND SHELTER FOR BIRDS

In the days when woodlands were plentiful and ancient trees slowly decayed away over decades, birds used holes in the tree trunks as nesting sites, or other places hidden away in the dense undergrowth. Today, far fewer places exist for birds to nest, which is why it is considered by almost all wildlife organizations to be of paramount importance for people to put up nest boxes in their gardens, to replace the lost habitats birds once occupied.

There are two main types of box that birds readily nest in. One is the tit box, which is enclosed apart from a small hole and which may be used by blue tits, great tits, nuthatches or even wrens. The other popular type is an open nest box. This is used by birds such as robins and flycatchers.

Start thinking about putting up a nest box in early winter, some time before nesting begins, so that the birds have time to locate and get used to the site and are comfortable with it when nesting begins. Some birds such as blue tits or wrens will use the boxes for shelter and roosting during the winter.

Positioning a nest box carefully may mean the difference between success and failure at attracting birds. Tit boxes need to be put somewhere sheltered from full sun, or the eggs or chicks will die of

From the humblest of home-made homes to a pretty dovecote, birds appreciate being provided with shelters.

MAKING A SMALL-HOLE NEST BOX

A nest box is best made out of wood, with hardwoods lasting longer. Choose a piece which is at least 15mm thick to provide insulation and prevent warping and 150mm × 1170mm.

1. Draw out the measurements shown, onto the plank.

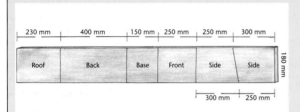

2. Using a saw, cut out the pieces. Then drill a hole in the front piece, depending on the size of birds that are already in your area: 25mm for blue, coal and marsh tit, 28mm for a great tit and tree sparrow, or 32mm for a house sparrow. Mark on the edge of the roof where the hinges are to go.

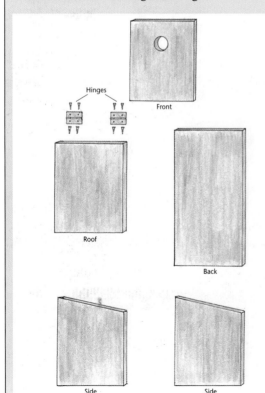

3. Drill some small drainage holes in the floor of the nest.

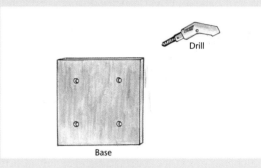

4. Nail or screw all the pieces together, except the roof, which should be fitted with a waterproof hinge or a nailed-down butyl strip, so that access is available for cleaning.

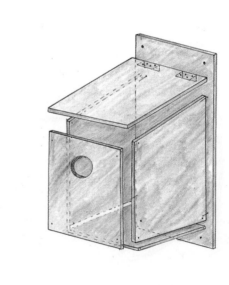

The outside of the box can be treated with a wood-based preservative but this must not be used on the inside and should be left for some time after treatment before being put up for use.

over-heating. Tree trunks or walls are suitable sites. An open-fronted box needs to be concealed behind climbing plants on a wall or fence, or secured to a hedge.

When the birds have finished nesting you can clear out the nest box. Be sure to check that the box is empty, as the residents may decide to have a second, late family, which won't appreciate being disturbed. By the winter it is safe to clean out the box. It is extremely important to do this each year to keep the facilities clean and pest free for the next residents, as birds harbour a variety of parasites. Wearing rubber gloves, scrub the box thoroughly with soapy water.

Whichever box you choose, think carefully about making sure the position is out of the way of cats and other predators and preferably as high as possible off the ground. Don't put nest boxes too close to each other, as birds like space from their neighbours so there is enough room for all of them to gather food close to the nesting site. If you find a box hasn't been used after a couple of years, the position may not be suitable, so move it to another part of the garden.

Making boxes

Although painted boxes can look very pretty, birds prefer the natural look of wood, which blends into the background and is what they would prefer in the wild. It is important not to use any stains, toxic paints or wood protection materials as these may be toxic to the birds, so natural boxes are the best. Make sure that whatever design you create, you have a hinged lid, so the box can easily be cleaned.

Nesting materials

If you clear up every leaf and twig in your garden, the birds will struggle to find nesting material in the locality. An old feather pillow can be cut open and used to provide plenty of material for birds to feather their nests. If you have a friendly hairdresser, the cuttings from the salon floor are also ideal for birds' nests.

Using moss killer on the lawn means removing a source of material used by birds such as finches

in their nests, so it is better for wildlife to allow it to grow. Near the pond, an accessible, muddy area will be useful for birds that need to pick up mud to glue their nests together.

Providing shelter for birds

As well as nest boxes, birds need places to shelter in bad weather and to roost at night. Some birds such as collared doves roost in trees. Starlings may use buildings as a sort of makeshift tree but providing good areas of shelter is an area in which gardeners can greatly help our feathered friends.

Many small birds will use hedging or shrubs for shelter and will particularly like dense branch structure that they can hide within. In the winter,

The feathers from an old pillow and other nesting materials can be left in a hanging basket for the birds to use.

*A tangle of Traveller's joy (*Clematis vitalba*) left to its own devices offers summer cover for birds and has the added attraction of seedheads.*

GOOD PLANTS FOR BIRD COVER

*The Yew tree (*Taxus baccata*) provides berries which are edible for birds but poisonous to humans and livestock. This ancient evergreen also provides year-round shelter for birds.*

With all of the following the Latin name refers to the common or native species but most cultivars will also work for cover.

Ivy (*Hedera helix*)
Honeysuckle (*Lonicera periclymenum*)
Clematis (*Clematis vitalba*)
Yew (*Taxus baccata*)
Holly (*Ilex aquifolium*)
Pine (*Pinus sylvestris*)

evergreen trees and shrubs are a lifeline to provide shelter for birds, so even if you haven't got the space to add an evergreen tree such as a conifer, a prickly evergreen shrub such as holly will be a great help and also adds colour and structure to the winter garden. Some varieties of cypress provide a good, dense cover for birds and can be used as ornamental trees or just as hedging.

Don't be tempted to explore hedging for nests, as this is the quickest way to scare the birds away from it, leaving the chicks to die. If you want to look at a nest, wait until the winter for a quick peek and if you are not sure who was living in your 'hedge hotel', look at the shape and materials used in the nest and a bird guide will reveal who the visitors were, which may help you plan to grow plants to help feed those particular species.

Tempting though it may be to clear up a tangle of clematis, honeysuckle or ivy, these climbers can also provide vital cover for birds who may nest inside it or use it for shelter from predators. With all these potential nesting and roosting sites, it is very important to delay pruning until later in the summer when the fledglings have gone.

COPING WITH A CASUALTY

From time to time an injured bird may appear in the garden and if it is seriously injured it may well be kindest to end its misery. However, birds can often simply be stunned by flying into a glass window pane. A bird who is stunned may just require half an hour's rest, protected from predators, so if it is possible to provide a warm, safe haven for the bird while it recovers, this may help. It is possible to buy special stickers to put on large picture windows, so the birds see that it is a solid barrier.

Fledglings fallen from the nest are a regular, heart-rending sight but they are best left alone, as their parents may still be feeding them even if they are out of the nest and may just be away getting food. If humans handle or feed the fledglings, the parents may well abandon them.

The best thing to do is let the birds get on with it, keeping any pets such as cats indoors until the fledgling has been encouraged to fly. If in any doubt about how to treat a sick bird, it is really best to seek expert help from your local wildlife trust or the RSPB.

There may also be local experts who can advise on how to look after a sick bird and are often easier to get hold of than some of the bigger organizations. Keeping a note of their phone number where you can find it easily when an accident occurs will save valuable time if you find a bird or any other wild animal in distress.

ATTRACTING OWLS

Whether or not you can attract owls into your garden may mainly depend on your location. Tawny owls need to be next to woodland, and barn owls and little owls near farmland. Tawny owls are the most likely visitors, to a large garden with mature deciduous trees. The best you can do for owls is to keep large trees and not poison rodents, particularly mice, as this is what they eat.

It is possible to install special owl nest boxes if you are in an area that could house them. The nests of owls, which would previously have been in the cavities of old trees or abandoned buildings, are less common these days, so providing nest boxes is essential.

Around half the population of barn owls now live in nest boxes provided by humans, as so much of their previous habitat no longer exists. Tawny owls will also take to nest boxes, as do kestrels and doves. If you live somewhere with an outhouse or barn, which may once have had nesting owls, contact a wildlife organization and they will advise on the best places and type of nest box to use to provide a home for the owls again.

CHAPTER 5

Welcome visitors

Plants are not the only things that can be encouraged to thrive in the garden: so can animals. There are a variety of mammals, up to thirty species, from the small and squeaky to the large and lumbering that will visit or live in our gardens. All have a place in the ecology of the world and we can expand our understanding of life through watching these wonderful creatures.

The larger the animal, the more likely it is to trample on your flower beds, but it is well worth putting up with a few squashed plants to enjoy seeing some of our bigger garden visitors. With so much land taken up by humans, we need to learn to take pleasure from sharing our space with creatures whose own habitats have often been destroyed.

BADGERS IN THE GARDEN

Secretive, splendid and adaptable, badgers bring joy and some consternation to the gardener in equal measure. It is a true delight to see badgers in the garden but they can sometimes be a little bit destructive in their search for food, or if you upset one of their pathways, so if you have badgers around, there may be some measures you need to take to get along together happily.

Badgers live in well-organized setts and are very much creatures of habit, living in the same territories for generations. If you have a sett in the garden, it must be left alone; badgers and their setts are

Animals such as badgers like to live in woodland away from humans. As many of their homes have been turned into farmland or built on, they are increasingly forced to visit or even live in gardens.

protected by the law. The best way to co-exist is to start to enjoy badger watching and not worry too much about the areas of the garden that they use. We all need to learn to share the land, rather than consider it the exclusive territory of humans and living with badgers around the garden is a good place to begin.

If you have badgers entering the garden, they will always use the same route so it should be easy to spot their well-worn pathways. If you have moved to a new property, or there are changes to your

Badgers are particularly partial to soft fruit and may well be attracted to your garden if you grow them.

current land, this may cause difficulties if you are blocking off established badger routes. To prevent damage to fences, it is best to leave the route open, or fit a special badger gate (a bit like a cat flap) that the badgers can use, as they may only be crossing your garden.

As they are nocturnal, badgers can often pass through their feeding grounds unseen. Often the first sign of a badger visiting the garden is the appearance of shallow pits in the lawn. These are caused when they forage for invertebrates such as leatherjackets, the larvae of the crane-fly. Damage to turf is most likely in dry conditions, when food (such as earthworms) is not on the surface, and is usually short lived, mostly in the late autumn and early spring.

Badgers are omniverous and are also partial to strawberries, raspberries and other soft fruit. They will also hope to share your harvest of vegetables such as carrots, potatoes and sweetcorn. In the flower garden, they may dig up bulbs to eat. To prevent damage to the latter, one solution is to lay wire netting beneath the soil, to protect the bulbs.

If you have particularly precious plants or don't want to share your fruit and vegetables, try to grow these in an area away from the badgers' routes and use barriers to keep badgers away. This can be very strong and high chain fencing, or (in the last event) an electric fence around the area. As this is all rather desperate, it may be better to learn to accept that a certain amount of damage is inevitable. Or better still, why not grow some fruit especially for the badgers and see if you can spot them eating it? If you still have concerns, your local wildlife trust will be able to give you help and advice.

Badgers also sometimes dig in lawns to make latrines but as this is seasonal – most noticeable in the spring and a little bit in the autumn – tolerance is the best solution.

Whether or not it is right to feed badgers is a debatable point. They are wild mammals and it is not good for them to become over-dependent on artificial sources of food. However, as houses are built over more and more land, badgers are losing natural food sources. In winter and spring, or during very dry, hot spells, when they can't easily get at worms and grubs on the surface of the soil, feeding them occasionally may actually prevent them damaging the garden. Of course, it may also attract even more badgers into the garden.

It may also be possible to lure badgers away from digging up precious plants if they are being fed in another part of the garden. If you are feeding birds or squirrels with peanuts or peanut butter, this may attract badgers. The badgers may even be digging in the grass to raid caches of nuts that squirrels have put there. They can be fed wet dog or cat food, dry cat food with biscuits, fruit and unsalted nuts. Water should always be provided to prevent dehydration, which is one of the badger's biggest problems during periods of drought.

Badger watching can become an addiction and there are many local groups who take an interest in protecting and watching badgers and their setts. If you know they are there but cannot see them, CCTV can provide interesting footage of a whole world going on in your garden, which you never knew about. If you become interested in badgers it is worth joining one of the local badger watch groups to share your interest and find out more about these fascinating creatures.

THE FOXY GARDENER

Foxes are probably more commonly spotted in suburban gardens than in the countryside. Indeed, urban foxes tend to fare better than their country cousins, finding more sources of food. However life

Many animals, including badgers and foxes, will eat fallen fruit, so leave some of your harvest on the ground for them.

is not easy for the fox as it is unpopular with some people; although since they do very little harm to gardens, there is no reason why the wildlife gardener should not enjoy their visits. They are certainly amongst the most beautiful of our regular garden visitors.

Foxes may occasionally make a bit of a mess when digging a hole, to bury excess food for later, in the same way as a dog buries a bone, but this is infrequent behaviour. One of my allotment neighbours fed a vixen every evening with dog biscuits, which the fox would bury in little caches amongst the allotmenteer's potato crops, which he would find when harvesting the potatoes. The vixen was saving the biscuits for leaner times. However, the allotment holder swore the fox had gardening ambitions and was hoping the buried dog biscuits would grow to be a bumper crop, too.

Some people are unnerved by the eerie screams of the female fox on warm nights in January and February, as she calls for a mate, followed by rather noisy proceedings when the liaison begins. There

Foxes often live on allotment sites and will burrow under sheds to find a daytime resting place.

Growing plenty of autumn berries will attract birds and may bring badgers and foxes into the garden if they are in the locality.

isn't much that can be done about this and it is just as noisy if it is in your garden or somewhere along the road, so if it wakes you at night it may be better to treat it as an opportunity to quietly observe the foxes while they are too busy to care.

Foxes mark their territory with their scent and their faeces. An acrid smell of fox urine, especially first thing in the morning, or after rain, may be the first way in which you notice you have a fox visiting the garden. The faeces, which look like thin rope which is twisted, has a wisp of hair at the pointed end. Foxes tend to leave their faeces in prominent places for territorial marking.

Foxes can burrow under sheds if there is a gap of about 12cm or more, or sometimes under fences. In fact finding somewhere to rest in the daytime is often the most difficult challenge for foxes in well-manicured gardens, so leaving an area with plenty of cover is the best way to attract them. If you don't mind the gap under your shed and there is sufficient surrounding cover, a vixen may choose to make it into a den where cubs can be reared.

If you do end up with cubs, they might cause damage to some plants, as they roll around playing and making a yikkering sound in the garden in late evening and at night in the early summer. The best advice is to protect precious plants, or move them to another area of the garden. However, the absolute delight to be had watching them more than compensates for a few squashed plants.

Foxes are omnivores and in urban situations will often scavenge in unsecured bins. For foxes, hedgehogs and other wildlife it is very important not to leave any food tins around as they commonly get their snouts stuck in them, causing terrible distress and injury. They also eat beetles and in the autumn they will eat fallen fruit, so the gardener can help them by leaving some of the crop for them. They will eat rabbits and rodents so they can be useful pest controllers, although they can eat birds (including of course domestic chickens) and pet rabbits.

If you keep chickens, guinea pigs or rabbits, securing their housing to be fox-proof is vital in order to prevent an attack. It may even be worth considering whether or not to keep these animals if you are in an area that is frequented by foxes as it can cause a lot of heartache. The idea that foxes kill 'for pleasure' is now being challenged; it has been suggested that they simply overkill and in a natural environment where the dead animals are not removed, they would return to their larder at a later date when their other food supplies were running short.

If you wish to attract foxes to your garden, the best way is to provide areas of cover, grow plenty of autumn fruit and have a source of water. They can also be fed with any scraps, or dog food, if the local cats or other animals don't get to it first; this may also attract badgers. It is possible to have badgers, foxes and cats all together in a garden but there is a firm pecking order: cats with attitude are at the top of the tree and foxes are at the bottom, although a nervous cat may suddenly remember things it has to do back inside the safety of its home.

Watching foxes is a delight but if you really don't want them around, there are repellents that can deter them and the best policy is to find the point of entry into the garden and place, for example, citronella-based special pellets at that point. Remember, however, that foxes are not easily put off if your garden is in their territory and fencing and walls are not a deterrent as they can easily jump up and over them. Perhaps a fox in the garden is a good reminder that wildlife will enter our gardens whether we like it or not.

THE GARDENER'S FRIEND

A strange snuffling and rustling around a hedge may herald the arrival of a hedgehog in the garden. Beloved by the gardener for its ability to hoover up slugs, having a hedgehog visiting, or better still living in the garden is considered a great blessing. As a nocturnal animal, a little perseverance may be required to spot this garden visitor. Apart from the mysterious noises, the droppings, about 5cm long and full of insects, may be another give-away.

The ancestors of these extraordinary little creatures were sniffing around about 15 million years ago, so they are supreme survivors. As the 'hedge' bit of their name suggests, they like to bustle around at the bottom of hedges and on rough grassland but have also learned to adapt to less suitable gardens, with a little help from their gardening friends. Providing hedging for shelter is therefore the first thing a gardener can do to help the hedgehog. Given the right conditions, your prickly friend can live for about seven years, plenty of time to get acquainted.

Hedgehogs can be found in overgrown areas of the garden, so it is worth allowing the grass to grow long in some areas to offer them areas of shelter.

Hedgehogs may be found in any overgrown areas and are therefore sometimes victims of strimmers or mowers, which often mutilate them. If you are using a strimmer on high vegetation, cut it down first to about one foot above the ground, then check for hedgehogs or other wildlife before cutting it any lower. Although shy, hedgehogs have rather bad eyesight, so will often let you get quite close to them, providing you don't move suddenly.

Housing a hedgehog

As hedgehogs hibernate, in autumn they start to gather suitable material to make a nest in anticipation of the winter ahead. They will use leaves and grass in particular to make a cosy nest, so it is important not to sweep up leaves early in the winter, if they must be swept up at all.

The kind of location they will seek out, apart from under a hedge, is often under a pile of material such as logs or brushwood. If it is possible to create such an area and leave it undisturbed, this is ideal, especially if it starts to grow mosses and algae, which in turn will attract insects. Unfortunately, hedgehogs are also attracted to hibernate under bonfires. Ideally, it is better to use a proper incinerator for a fire, or check the pile very carefully before starting a fire, or move it to a different position before setting it alight. A mass of pampas grass also needs checking for nesting hogs before burning or trimming.

The bottom of an undisturbed compost heap makes a warm, dark cosy place to build a nest, therefore it is essential to take great care when turning the heap as a fork can easily kill baby hedgehogs. This is best done around October or November at the latest, as at this time the adults

A well-built hedgehog home, situated in undergrowth in a quiet area of a garden, will provide waterproof shelter during hibernation.

have yet to go into hibernation and the year's young hedgehogs should have left home.

Ready-made hedgehog houses can be bought or made, although the most important contribution you can make to their welfare if at all possible is to provide the materials and shelter the hedgehogs need to create their own winter nest, called a hibernaculum. If you make your own hedgehog house, it needs to be very strong and is most inviting if covered with earth and wood. It also needs to have a special entrance.

Place the house somewhere protected, near or under plant cover, perhaps at the base of a wall or fence in an area where it will not be disturbed, away from the house. There is no need to put nesting materials in it, as they might not suit the hedgehog and it will be happy to decide on its own soft furnishing arrangements, gathering leaves as part of its winter hibernation ritual. Once the 'sold' sign has gone up outside the house, resist the temptation to disturb it. Female hedgehogs can abandon the nest, leaving their young in it, if they are frightened.

It is no wonder the hedgehog seems to have a busy nocturnal diary. Hedgehogs munch their way through around a hundred slugs, caterpillars, beetles and insect larvae every night. This means a balanced garden, which has attracted plenty of insects and has places for them to breed, is ideal for the hedgehog. Slug pellets should never be used around hedgehogs. Some types of pellets are poisonous to them, others enter the food chain because the slugs die and are left on the earth's surface.

It is far, far better to protect delicate plants with cloches until they grow big enough to be less attractive to slugs and snails, than to attempt to wipe out the enemy. After all, you are not just endangering the humble hedgehog but also removing one of its important food sources.

If you wish to supplement your hedgehog's diet, they appreciate tinned dog or cat food, or you can now buy commercial hedgehog feed, or mealworms. Traditionally people gave them milk and bread but they can't digest lactose and it is now thought that a frequent diet of this may cause them considerable suffering.

A few bowls of water should always be dotted about for them, especially when supplying food. During hibernation, hedgehogs wake up every

MAKING A HOME FOR A HEDGEHOG

There are designs available for making wooden hedgehog homes but this is the simplest method.

1. Buy or make a sturdy wooden crate. Turn it upside down.

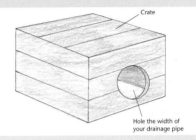

2. Using a piece of drainage pipe, cut a hole in the bottom of the crate that the pipe will fit into neatly to prevent predators.

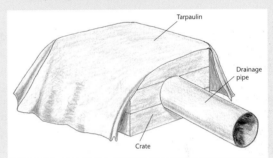

3. Fit the pipe to the crate, leaving it sticking out, and then cover the crate with a tarpaulin or other waterproof material.

4. Then cover this with leaves, earth, branches and logs, so that it ends up looking like a log pile.

Slug pellets can kill hedgehogs, who will eat the poisoned slugs, so it is far better to consider protecting plants against slugs and snails.

couple of weeks. If you see them foraging around, this may be a particularly good time to provide them with food and water as they lose their fat reserves through the winter and need to save energy instead of searching out water.

It is always worth leaving plants standing through the winter where possible, rather than neatening up the garden too much, as they will not only provide seed heads for birds but attract overwintering insects which the hedgehogs feed on.

It may also be an interesting experiment to see if a visiting hedgehog finds any of your plants attractive for the purpose of self-anointing. This is a strange aspect of their behaviour, where the animal licks its spines in a froth of scented saliva, the scent taken from a strong-smelling plant. The purpose of this is arguable, but if it finds an unusual, usually highly aromatic or acrid aroma in your garden, it may choose to anoint its spines with it, a strange activity in which it becomes totally absorbed, giving you a good chance to observe it.

NIGHT FLYERS IN THE GARDEN

There are about seventeen species of native bats, of which around five can be seen in gardens at dusk or on a moonlit night. If you have bats in your garden, this may indicate that you have started to achieve a good balance for wildlife, as they do not survive well in areas where chemicals are used and dislike disturbance.

Bats feed by catching insects on the wing and are helpful in reducing mosquitoes and midges in a garden. They also eat many nocturnal moths as they hunt at night, eating up to a hundred insects an hour. Flowers and vegetables may breathe a sigh of relief at the presence of bats, as they often eat insects whose larvae cause damage to plants.

Bats hibernate in winter, using holes in trees, caves or roof spaces in old buildings. Their habitats have been reduced, partly due to fewer natural habitats being available to the bat and partly due to the use of insecticides killing their food sources. Several species of bats are consequently endangered species.

Bat boxes are sometimes erected by people to offer them a new home. The success of this is rather limited, in that having a bat box will not necessarily attract bats to your garden if they do not consider it the right habitat, but there is no harm in putting a box in an out-of-the-way place, high up a tree, close to woodland if there is any nearby. Then at least they have the possibility of using it, should they so choose.

Bats particularly like a roost site near to areas such as hazel woods or coniferous woodland so if you don't have this nearby, you may not be able to offer them a permanent home. However, bats will sometimes use a box temporarily. It can in fact take years before a box is occupied.

Bats are also very fussy, so they are unlikely to visit any leaky old box erected on their behalf, so the wood and cement type, such as a Schwegler box, is more useful. Look for droppings below the box to see if it is being used. If you do make a wooden box, do not use any preservatives, as this will be fatal to the bats.

If bats aren't keen on the box you provide, they will nevertheless appreciate a good source of water and plenty of flowers and native hedgerows to attract the insects they feed on.

As they are declining in number, it is illegal to kill, disturb or unnecessarily handle a bat, or to destroy or obstruct its roost, even when the roost is not in use, as bats tend to return to sites every year. If their roosting, for example in a roof, causes a serious problem, an organization such as the Wildlife Trust or Bat Conservation Trust will be able to give advice on the subject.

SLOW-WORMS

If you lift up an area of ground-cover fabric, or some logs that have been lying around for some time, you may well find yourself surprising a slow-worm. Its name will soon become clear – as a cold-blooded reptile, it takes a while to heat up and so when disturbed from snoozing in a hiding place it often takes a few minutes to rev up, during which time you can observe this interesting creature at close quarters.

It isn't actually a worm at all, or a snake, although it looks rather like one; it is a legless lizard. It is distinguishable from a snake in that as a lizard it has eyelids, which snakes lack (so if it winks at you, you know it's a slow-worm, not a snake). A good gardener will draw back a bit of shelter to show you his or her slow-worms with pride. This is because slow-worms get on very well with wildlife garden-ers. Apart from eating worms, spiders and the ubiquitous woodlouse, slow-worms have a penchant for slugs, particularly white slugs, which they will often swallow without even chewing them first. If that isn't enough to keep the gardener happy, they will also suck snails out of their shells and make a meal out of them, too.

The slow-worm looks like a snake but is actually a legless lizard.

A log pile will give slow-worms a place to hide and hunt out food such as woodlice.

Slow-worms, like all British reptiles, are a pro-tected species and are under threat as their natural habitat of rough grassy areas, moors and heath-land diminishes. If you are lucky enough to live in an area with slow-worms, as a wildlife gardener you can help keep the population going with a little consideration.

As with other wildlife, slow-worms benefit from a pile of logs for them to hide beneath and some long grass where they can slither about and hunt for slugs. A bit of old dark ground-cover material or something similar will provide a place under which they can warm up. They may use a warm compost heap to breed in, so as with hedgehogs, take great care when turning compost. As they burrow under soil, as deep as 30cm, also check if you are going to disturb them if you are clearing ground that has not recently been cultivated. Take care when mowing longer grass or consider cutting it on a higher setting to prevent injury or death.

Two other members of the lizard family, the sand and common lizard, are relatively uncommon in the garden, unless the area is close to their normal habitat. Lizards are not harmful.

SNAKES IN THE GRASS

The snake you are most likely to come across in a British garden is the grass snake, which can grow up to 1.8m in length. The easiest way to identify it is by the yellow collar, with a black edge, which is just behind the head. Snakes are attracted to ponds and will happily denude the population of frogs, newts and fish in and around the pond. They will also make a meal of small mammals, ground-nesting birds and their eggs. Like all other British reptiles, they are protected by the Wildlife Act. The grass snake is not venomous, but it can bite so it should not be handled.

The base of an old tree trunk makes the perfect hiding spot for a grass snake.

Apart from at the pond side, the other place the wildlife gardener might encounter the grass snake is in the compost bin, or a nice warm pile of manure that is rotting down. Here, they lay eggs in early summer, so once again, if you know you have grass snakes, it is important to take care when turning compost as the eggs can easily get destroyed or exposed to the cold, killing them. Adders, our only venomous snake, only very rarely visit gardens, if the gardens back on to their ordinary habitats. However, they very rarely bite unless handled.

AN UNUSUAL GUEST

One delightful garden visitor that you will only come across if you live in some areas in the north of England and parts of Scotland is the pine marten. It was once established in British woodlands and is related to the stoat and the weasel.

This charming creature is tempted to gardens where there is food left out. If you live in an area where they exist (which will probably be on the edge of a wood or forest) you may want to encourage them into the garden. They are very shy and it takes patience to get them to visit a garden regularly but it is well worth it to witness these very appealing creatures.

LESS WELCOME VISITORS

Not all garden visitors are welcomed by the gardener, but it must always be remembered that they are part of a complex natural order and may provide food for other predators or have useful predation skills themselves.

Rodents

Rats will be attracted by any leftovers lying around, so use trays below bird feeders to prevent leaving scraps on the ground if you find them a problem. They may climb up wooden bird feeders but are less likely to try to get up the sort of metal poles that are available, so if you know you have rats, you may prefer to use the latter. If they are to be discouraged, it may be necessary to stop feeding birds for a while, particularly avoiding scattering food on the ground. Take care not to put meat, dairy products, eggs, or cooked foods into the compost heap.

Mice will dig up bulbs, so if you know they are around, it might be worth trying the technique (also effective against squirrels and badgers) of planting the bulbs, then laying chicken wire over them, and putting earth over that. The bulbs grow through the wire but can't be so easily dug up.

More simply, try moving bulbs to another part of the garden which may not be so badly affected. Remember bulbs in storage are a great temptation, so bulbs left in sheds or other outhouses need to be protected from tiny teeth. In the ground, a row

of peas that never surfaces may have been eaten by mice; these too can be protected with wire over the surface.

Of course there is no reason not to embrace or at least tolerate rodents and some people even create feeding stations for wood mice and voles; the latter can sometimes be spotted feeding during the day. However, rodents carry some bacterial infections which are transferable to humans, such as leptospirosis (also known as Weil's disease), so it is a good precaution to wear disposable or rubber gloves when cleaning an area that might attract mice and voles, particularly if you have any broken skin on your hands. With rats in particular, make sure they have no entry points into your home, as sharing

Mice and squirrels will readily dig up bulbs to eat but can be deterred by laying chicken wire over the bulbs when planting.

a house with rodents is perhaps a step too far from sharing the garden with wildlife.

Foxes or badgers, as well as cats, may act as informal pest controllers, if they come across any rodents. Country gardens with a strong population of mice and voles may also attract stoats and weasels, as well as birds of prey flying in for a quick snack. Ironically, rats, which we tend to be the most keen to dispose of, are actually effective predators of house mice.

Problems with insects

Wasps are not always welcome in case they try to nest near the house or in a roof space. If you want to discourage them, the easiest way to try to keep a balance in the garden is by encouraging insect-eating birds such as starlings, or blackbirds, which will eat them. Putting ripe fruit in an unused part of the garden will also draw them away from the house.

There are many harmless insects, such as the solitary mason bee, which use our buildings to create their nests. However, they do no harm and do not swarm, so it is worth checking exactly what species a creature is before eliminating it or destroying a nest. There are several insects that look similar to wasps but are completely harmless.

The persistent squirrel

When it comes to a free meal, no one can fault the squirrel's persistence. This bright-eyed, bushy-tailed rodent will learn and remember every which way

Squirrels are fast learners, and will soon work out where best to find a free meal. (Photo: Dawn Lewis)

Squirrels will eat nuts which may have been meant for birds. This may be a nuisance but they are just trying to survive too.

to get at nuts and other goodies. If you feed birds and have squirrels in your area, the chances are, the squirrels will hop along for a free meal, too.

If they are eating all the bird food, it may be an idea to provide a special squirrel feeder. This is a box with a lid that opens. Only the squirrel can prise it open, so while it is occupied with chomping its way through the contents, the birds can feed in peace. It is also rat-proof. Good food for squirrels includes unsalted peanuts, walnuts, almonds, hazelnuts and apples. Remember, though, that feeding these mammals should only be supplementary to their diet, otherwise they become too dependent on being fed.

If you live in one of the few areas with red squirrels, they can be encouraged particularly with pine cone seeds, fruit and berries. Make sure all feeders are kept clean and it is best not to encourage grey and red squirrels together because the grey squirrels carry the parapox virus, which kills the reds. As can be witnessed in many parks, squirrels will quickly learn to feed from your hand.

As with mice, bulbs and corms can be protected by burying them below chicken wire and putting soil on top to cover the wire. Squirrels can also strip bark, which may need protecting with a tree guard at the first sign of damage.

If you find squirrels a nuisance, protecting bulbs and tree bark are the best measures to take. There is little point in trying to get rid of them, as a vacant territory will simply be filled by a new gang; so it is worth learning to enjoy watching their extraordinary agility. After all, the squirrel is not, as we tend to imagine, simply being naughty or cheeky. It is simply trying to survive.

Making a mountain out of a molehill

The unassuming mole is sometimes despised by lovers of a perfect lawn, due to the molehills that can suddenly appear, caused by its subterranean excavations. It is hard to spot a mole, as it spends most of its time in its network of tunnels, which it can create at a rate of 20m a day. The freshly aerated soil that is thrown up as a result of this can be useful to the gardener.

The chances are, if you have moles and try to dispose of them, then more will move into the vacant plot, so it is better to tolerate them in a domestic situation. In fact, as well as eating worms, moles will eat slugs, leatherjackets and cutworms, controlling these pests on the gardener's behalf. If they are really making a mess of the lawn, maybe it is time to rethink whether or not you need such a big expanse of grass in the garden, and instead plant up the area with some of the wildlife-friendly shrubs and trees mentioned in this book, or turn it into a wildflower meadow, where the molehills won't be so noticeable.

Destructive deer

Deer, delightful as they are, are really not suitable garden visitors unless you have a very, very large garden indeed as they can be very destructive. Gardens near woodland may attract Fallow deer; otherwise it will be Muntjac, Sika or Roe deer, the last being the most likely to visit a garden. They may find ways in through holes in hedges, or jump over low fences.

Deer will quickly demolish shrubs, rose beds and vegetables, particularly in spring or early summer. The tell-tale signs of visiting deer, apart from damage to plants, is their distinctive hoof print, called a slot. The size of this will indicate which type of deer it is.

Rabbits

Perhaps surprisingly, in a large garden, rabbits can be useful, keeping grass both cropped and fertilized with droppings. However, in a smaller garden, rabbits can cause havoc fairly fast, because as well as grass, they will munch their way through a vegetable patch and on tree bark.

If rabbits get into your garden, the only solution is to put up fencing that is dug several feet into

Fallow deer may visit gardens on the edge of woodland to forage for food. (Photo: A.J. Hunt)

Fencing is the only way to deter rabbits from eating crops in an allotment or garden.

the ground, to stop them burrowing underneath it.

If fencing off a whole area is impractical, then wire fencing can be used to protect special plants and it may be worth finding plants that are of less interest to the average bunny. If the rabbits cannot be kept at bay, sprinkling Epsom salts around plants may deter them. Hares, with longer legs and black-tipped ears, are not a nuisance, as they are very rarely seen in gardens, preferring to eat grasses in open fields.

CHAPTER 6

Water for wildlife

Having a constant source of water in the garden is probably one of the most important features you can create to help maintain an ecological balance and attract wildlife. Ideally, this involves creating a pond for wildlife. However, if your garden doesn't have the space for a pond, it is still possible to provide areas of water in containers. This will still attract some passing creatures but may not offer them breeding grounds.

POSITIONING A POND

Position the pond in a predominantly sunny spot, on a level site. It will warm up more quickly, freeze less frequently and facilitate the growth of plants. From an aesthetic point of view, it also adds value in terms of creating more reflections from the sun and sky. Make sure there are no trees overhanging the pond, as dead leaves will pile up in the pond and create noxious gases, which reduce the oxygen available.

Look at the space from a variety of angles, especially from inside the house, and upstairs, so that you make sure the pond will be in a position that you like. A pond can become a great focal point in a garden, or just be tucked away in a quiet corner. Not all creatures will want to be centre-stage, so putting the pond too close to the house or in a busy spot in the garden may discourage some visitors.

Wherever it is, a pond will provide hours of interest as you watch the wildlife come and go and you can be sure that you are adding a feature that

will be of benefit to many creatures as well as providing great pleasure for yourself.

Children love ponds and pond dipping and it is a great way for them to learn about some of the aquatic creatures that live alongside us. However, it is important that the pond has some sort of a grid covering as even shallow water can be dangerous if a child falls into it. If protection of a pond is not viable, it might be better to settle for a bog garden until the children are a little older.

TYPES OF POND

Ponds can be formal, in a geometric shape such as a circle or square, or made into a more natural, irregular type of shape. They can be made out of a variety of materials. When choosing what type of pond to create, it is worth considering what will best suit wildlife and will be durable.

A pond can be created out of any sort of container. A half-barrel or a frost-proof pot can be used to great effect to create a small area of still water in a specific area and display a few pond plants.

There are several ways in which a pond can be created and all of them will contribute to some extent in bringing wildlife into your garden. However, to attract wildlife other than insects, a pond ideally needs to have a shallow end, created by partly filling the container with rocks and pebbles or other material, to make one edge accessible to allow animals to get in and out.

From a flowing stream to the smallest of water features, all water is a vital resource in the garden for wildlife.

A very gently sloping 'beach' created at one end of a pond provides easier access to the water for birds and other small animals.

TYPES OF POND LINER

PVC and butyl liners

Both PVC and butyl rubber are flexible materials, which make them good for a natural pond. PVC is a thick, elastic type of polythene. It is cheaper than butyl but not as long lasting and can degrade quite rapidly under sunlight. Butyl rubber is flexible and strong and lasts for many years, and is therefore the best choice for a wildlife pond. It can be moulded to create the right shapes for a natural-looking pond.

Glass fibre liners

These are strong, rigid and manufactured in pre-formed shapes. Fitting one is fairly simple, in that it just requires a hole to be dug and then backfilled with sand or soil to support it. However, it can be quite tricky as the hole needs to be exactly the same shape as the pond liner, or it will not lie flat on the soil.

Concrete ponds

Concrete may be useful for some types of formal ponds but it can fracture and get leaks due to water expansion in ice, or soil shifting. It also contains lime, which is toxic to wildlife and fish. There are products that can be painted on to protect aquatic animals from the lime but they must be left to dry for an adequate amount of time before introducing any living creatures into the pond.

Clay pools

In areas with underlying clay, it is possible to create an entirely natural pond by digging a hole and creating a skin of at least 20cm out of the clay. However, the clay needs to be completely free of any sand or stones and carefully worked to get the right plasticity to make it watertight. If you are

happy to experiment, it is an interesting method to try and has the advantage of only using natural materials. However as leaks may cause problems, other methods of lining ponds are favoured for guaranteed results.

Recycled pond materials

Recycling an old bath, sunk into the ground and partly filled with stones to make one end accessible to wildlife, is ideal and an idea often used on allotments. Even an old butler-style sink makes a pleasing container for a miniature pond. Ingenuity in making a pond out of a discarded object can add a pleasingly quirky touch to the garden.

Where space is short, an old half barrel container can be used to make an unusual water feature which will still attract insects.

> ### HOW TO MEASURE FOR A FLEXIBLE POND LINING
>
> 1. Measure the length for the pond at its maximum length, then the width at its maximum. Decide on the maximum depth required.
> 2. Write down the length, then add on twice the depth. This gives you the total length.
> 3. To calculate the width, write down the width, then add on twice the depth measurement again, to get the total width.
>   For example, a small pond is to be 2m long, 1.5m wide and 0.5m deep.
>   So the calculation is:
>   2m (length) + 1m (depth × 2) = 3m length
>   1.5m (width) + 1m (depth × 2) = 2.5m length.
>   The total area of the liner required is therefore 3m × 2.5m.
>
> Allow at least 30cm extra for edging when placing, to be trimmed off later. It is always better to have too much liner than to discover that you have too little too late. If you are still struggling, some pond liner distributors on the Internet have calculators that will do the sums for you, or the shop selling the liner may be able to help.

MAKING A POND WITH A FLEXIBLE LINER

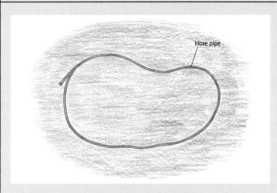

1. Once the site has been chosen, the pond should be marked out using a piece of hose, or sand. First, measure the outline so that you know the maximum width and depth that you can go to and then mark the shape, which with wildlife ponds tends to be modelled on a natural pond, for example, a rough oval shape.

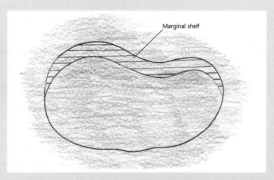

2. Next, mark in the area within the pond where you will be putting a shelf, which will accommodate marginal plants. This may run for half, or even almost all the way around the pond.
3. Choose which end of the pond will be the deep end, and then create a 'beach' at another part of the pond. Sharp shelving prevents many creatures from gaining access to the pond, so a 'beach' means an area where the water and the slope into it are shallow. This allows wildlife such as smaller birds to be able to get in and out of the water. This also means there is an area where the shallower water will warm up more quickly, which will suit spawn.
4. The pond should ideally have an area within it that is at least 1m deep. At this depth and below, the water will not freeze. This is vital for species that

remain in the pond throughout the year. Depth allows hibernating frogs to survive the winter and the pond is less likely to become clogged with algae. However, if this is not possible, any pond is better than no water in the garden and will still sustain some wildlife.

5. Remember before you start to dig to work out where you will put the excavated soil. It could be used to make a feature elsewhere in the garden. The topsoil is a valuable material for the garden. If you get down to the subsoil, this can be mixed with topsoil or you can dispose of it as it contains few nutrients.

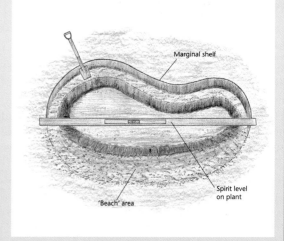

6. Dig out the shape, and create contouring margins. Use a spirit level balanced on a plank to establish that the edges are level. Pick out any sharp stones or any other material that could pierce the liner.

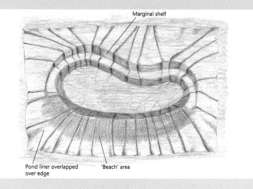

7. To protect the liner further, lay sand, newspaper, or a pond underlay (this can usually be bought from the pond supplier) in the hole. Put the liner in place with an overlap all around the edge. Fill the base of the pond with a little bit of topsoil, which will help plants to root. Then fill the deepest part of the pond with water. The butyl will stretch very slightly and you can then mould the liner around the contours, folding it where necessary to flatten it out around the edges. Fill up to the top, to check the level. You then need to leave it for a few hours, if possible, to allow the liner to stretch fully.

8. Finally, tuck the liner edge underneath the surrounding soil or stones to mask it. If you have dug the pond out of an area of lawn, some upturned turves will make a good edging and provide much-needed mud for nesting birds.

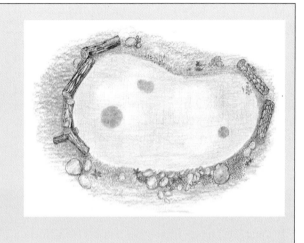

POND MAINTENANCE

In a new pond, an algae called blanket weed is likely to form as the pool establishes. There are special treatments that can be bought to reduce this, or more simply, just remove it by picking it up with a stick. Never throw away plant material taken from a pond immediately. Always place it temporarily at the pond's edge, so that any creatures hiding in the weed, plants or mud can return to the pond unharmed. Other algae will appear but it soon calms down as the pond life starts to feed on it.

Light may degrade any visible areas of a PVC liner and create holes. Animals can also create holes in liners. Butyl liners tend to be easier to repair but repair kits are available for both butyl and PVC liners.

The great thing about a wildlife pond is that it is fairly maintenance free but a small amount of care will help keep the pond healthy. Every few years, it is a good idea to remove about a third of the water and any debris. Fallen leaves should be picked off wherever they are visible. The reason for this is that as they decay they let off gases that are poisonous to some creatures. Some vigorous plants will need thinning over time.

It is best to avoid pond cleaning in the spring as amphibians may be breeding. If for some reason you have to clear out the pond completely, avoid doing so in winter, as creatures may be hibernating at the bottom of it. Autumn is therefore the best time for clearing operations.

If the pond freezes in winter, one simple act that will help anything living in the pond is to put an inflatable ball in the pond. This absorbs some of the pressure of the ice and the float can be removed to allow air under the ice. An alternative method is to put a pan of hot water on the surface of the ice until it melts a hole that will be sufficient to allow the pond to breathe again. Ice should never be smashed on a pond as this creates shock waves that can kill anything hibernating there.

POND LIFE

The first inhabitants of any pond are likely to be insects, which will draw in the larger creatures, particularly amphibians. The most common mini-creatures include pond skaters, water beetles, caddis-flies, snails, mayflies and the lovely damsel- and dragonflies. If you become interested in finding out more about the smaller inhabitants of your pond, there are pond-dipping courses available to adults as well as children, where experts are on hand to identify the huge variety of creatures you might come across.

You may be impatient waiting for the arrival of amphibians in your pond as it can take a couple of years for the habitat to suit them. However, don't be tempted to transfer spawn from another pond because you are keen to get them established. This can transfer diseases into your pond and the spawn may also not be sufficiently adapted to the environment you have to offer. It also takes time for the eco-system of your pond to develop and if you introduce amphibians too early there may not be enough food sources and areas of shelter established for them to survive. Allow the wildlife to decide for itself when your pond is suitable for habitation.

Frogs, toads and newts

For many of us, childhood was a time when we came face to face with the amphibian world, stirring up frogspawn, marvelling as they turned into tadpoles

The plants around the edges of a pond can provide year-round interest in the garden.

and then watching as they eventually turned into tiny frogs and hopped away. As adults, we tend to forget that in a world where their native habitats are often destroyed, we are still living alongside a variety of amphibians in our gardens.

Although frogs live on land, they return to water to breed and newts also need water in which to lay their eggs. Garden ponds are therefore a huge help to this small but significant part of the animal kingdom. Having them in the garden can mean we can legitimately revisit that childhood interest and introduce the next generation to the joys of the weird and wonderful world of amphibians. Of course, these creatures have the added benefit of being consumers of slugs and other unwanted plant pests.

There are three types of frog and toad, and three types of newt that are native to Britain. The former are the common frog, common toad and Natterjack toad. The frog is up to 10cm long with green- to brown-coloured smooth, moist skin, sometimes almost yellow with dark markings and a dark patch behind the eye. Frogs lay spawn in February and March, which become black tadpoles, turning mottled brown.

Toads are distinguishable from frogs by their warty skin and bulbous gland behind their eyes. The males grow up to 8cm but the females can be up to 13cm in length. The Natterjack toad is endangered in Britain and most commonly seen in a handful of sites, particularly the sand dunes on the northwest coast of England and the start of

Garden ponds can provide a safe haven in which frogs can lay their spawn. (Photo: Sally Cunningham)

Plant cover is essential to provide areas where pond life can breed.

hibernate under mud at the bottom of ponds and tick over by drawing in oxygen through their skin. However, if the pond freezes a lot, noxious poisons build up under the surface, which will kill the frog. The depth of the pond is significant here: if there is a section that is 1m deep, this will prevent the pond from freezing completely and the frogs can sleep easily at the bottom of it.

Whether or not you have a pond, a compost heap and piles of old logs, which attract insects, will provide a summer residence for frogs and attract some of their favourite insects as a food source.

Britain has three newt species: the smooth, the palmate, and the crested newt. The smooth (or common) newt is generally brown but during the breeding season, of March to May, the male develops a wavy black-spotted crest along the back and tail. Both males and females have a yellow to orange belly and spotted throats. They can grow to around 8 to 10cm. The palmate newt is similar in size and colour to the smooth newt, but without spots on its throat. Its webbed hind feet give it its name.

The great crested newt is also called a wart newt, due to its rough dark to black skin, patterned with small white spots. Like common newts it has an orange or yellow belly but it is the larger, growing up to 15cm. This species is on the decline. Great crested newts need areas of damp undergrowth for shelter as well as a pond.

Scotland, and in East Anglia and Lincolnshire. It is easily distinguished from the common toad by the yellow stripe that runs down the centre of its back and its habit of running, rather than crawling or hopping, like the common toad.

Unlike the familiar pile of frogspawn, toads produce strings of spawn. The common toad creates a double row of eggs, whereas the Natterjack toad makes a single row. The common toad's spawn appears in March or April but the Natterjack lays its single rows from April to as late as May. Like the frog's, the toad's tadpoles are black.

To attract amphibians to your pond, it needs to have certain features. As mentioned earlier, gentle slopes are important for all kinds of wildlife and shallow areas will be good for frogs spawning.

Although most frogs hide under the cover of logs or other suitable areas in winter, some male frogs

---

PROTECTED SPECIES

Great crested newts and Natterjack toads are both fully protected under the Wildlife and Countryside Act of 1981. This means that both the newts and their habitats can't be destroyed, damaged or disturbed. Even with their best interests in mind, neither they nor their spawn should be moved into a new pond. They are very specific in their habitat requirements, which is why they need protection. As newts lay their eggs on the curled leaves of aquatic plants, it is also important not to remove water plants from the wild, either, as you could be removing newts' eggs.

The common frog, toad and other types of newt also have limited protection: it is illegal to sell or advertise for sale the animals or their eggs or larvae. This prevents them being collected for the pet trade or laboratory use.

Logs placed in and around a pond can provide a summer shelter for frogs and the insects they feed on.

Fish in ponds

Many people like to have fish in ponds but for a wildlife pond it is really better to minimize the number or preferably have none at all, as they will munch their way through other kinds of wildlife, such as the eggs and tadpoles of newts and frogs. However, a pond with fish is better than no pond at all, so if you already have them you may have to accept that you will have fewer amphibians as a result. Many keen wildlife gardeners who keep fish end up creating two ponds, which can look very attractive – one for the wildlife and one for the fish.

Dragonflies

What can be more delightful than to see these ethereal creatures hovering over your pond? To attract a range of dragonflies and damselflies, a pond ideally needs to be at least 4m^2 in size, although a smaller pond will still attract some species. They need a mixture of plants growing submerged, floating and on the margins, where they can perch to lay their eggs, hunt and where their larvae can emerge. It is the larvae that demand such a large area of water; they feed on small creatures such as flea beetles and demand outstrips supply if the pond is too small.

*The delightful damselfly, here resting on a Royal fern (*Osmunda regalis*) will often frequent garden ponds in the summer months.*

*The delicate leaves of the butterfly fern (*Salvinia auriculata*), a free-floating pond plant which is frost tender but will create summer cover.*

*The leaves of the water lily (*Nymphaea spp.*) provide shade on the pond's surface and the flowers attract many insects.*

POND PLANTS

Plants look attractive in and around a pond and allow you to introduce a whole new range of plants into your garden. They are also vitally important for the wildlife in and around your pond, providing cover and areas for pond life to breed. Spring or early summer is the best time to get planting under way, as the water will be warming up and the plants grow most happily.

There are several types of pond plant: submerged (also called oxygenators), deep-water, floating and marginal plants. A wildlife pond requires a combination of all of these types of plant. Many plants can be divided and given to friends for their ponds but they need to be carefully washed and then left in a bucket of water for six weeks before being put into a new pond, to ensure that they are not carrying diseases or other unwanted pond weeds with them.

A pond's surface should eventually be about two-thirds aquatic plants to one-third clear water, so that this is the ratio you see on the pond's surface. If there is too little vegetation, there will not be enough habitats for wildlife and without some oxygenating plants it may not be possible to create a proper balance for all species. If on the other hand the vegetation takes over too much, filling the pond completely, this also creates problems as not enough light will reach the pond and it will eventually become more of a stale swamp. Getting it right isn't rocket science; it just requires choosing some plants from each of the following categories and planting them in the right place.

It may take a couple of years for the pond plants to get really established, so if you are thinking of having a pond, the sooner you get it going, the sooner you can enjoy it, knowing you are contributing to the welfare and survival of a mass of wildlife.

Submerged oxygenating plants

These plants usually grow up from the bottom of the pond and most break the surface of the water. They are vital for the wildlife pond, because their foliage gives off oxygen in tiny bubbles. They are also helpful because their roots use up nutrients that are too rich for ponds. When planting, weigh them down by tying them to a piece of stone or similar. Otherwise, they can be planted in baskets to control over-enthusiastic growth.

Hornwort (*Ceratophyllum demersum*)
Curled Pondweed (*Potamogeton crispus*)
Water Buttercup (*Ranunculus aquatilis*)

Floating aquatics

These do exactly that – they float on the surface of the pond and have fine roots that trail down into the water. Floating plants provide a habitat for some of the aquatic insects and the roots are useful cover for spawning fish. Planting couldn't be simpler – you just launch them onto the water and they will soon find their sea legs. In the autumn, the foliage breaks away and the seed pods sink to the bottom of the pond. Allow for floating aquatics to cover up to two-thirds of the pond's surface.

Water Chestnut (*Trapa natans*)
Water Hyacinth (*Eichhornia azurea*)
Water Soldier (*Stratiotes aloides*)
Frogbit (*Hydrocharis morsus-ranae*)

Hardy deep-water aquatics (with floating leaves)

These plants root in the mud at the bottom of the pond but have floating leaves. They are all useful plants and the lilies have pretty flowers and are best grown in the deepest part of the pond. Their leaves are useful to invertebrates as a place to lay eggs or larvae. Water lilies are great colonizers, developing dense rhizomatous root systems in the base of the pond, so it is necessary to cut them back from time to time to make sure some of the pond is clear of vegetation.

Pond Lily (*Nymphaea* spp.)
Yellow Pond Lily (*Nuphar lutea*)
Water Hawthorn (*Aponogeton distachyos*)

Marginals

Marginal plants provide height and form, and blur the pond's edging. Many also have very attractive

The flowering rush, Butomus umbellatus, *is a pretty marginal plant that attracts many insects.*

flowers. As the name suggests, they grow on the margin of the pond and in a wildlife pond this will usually mean on a shelf that has been created to house them. They prefer to have just a couple of inches of water around their roots. Special containers are available for marginal plants.

Flowering Rush (*Butomus umbellatus*)
Bog Arum (*Calla palustris*)
Marsh Marigold, Kingcup (*Caltha palustris*)
Yellow Iris (*Iris pseudacorus*)
Water Mint (*Mentha aquatica*)
Bog Bean, Buckbean, Marsh Trefoil (*Menyanthes trifoliata*)

Water Forget-me-not (*Myosotis scorpioides/palustris*)
Pickerel (*Pontederia cordata*)
Arrowhead (*Sagittaria sagittifolia*)
Brooklime (*Veronica beccabunga*)

Plants to avoid

Advice is often contradictory on what plants are best avoided in a pond. One thing to bear in mind is whether or not the pond is self-contained or will run into a waterway of any type. If it does, you need to think very carefully before introducing Canadian pondweed (*Elodea Canadensis*), as this is quite a thug and will take over very large areas very fast and has caused problems clogging up waterways such as canals. Others to avoid, which are usually rooted in mud, include New Zealand pygmy weed (*Crassula helmsii*) and Nuttall's pondweed (*Elodea nuttallii*). Floating pennywort (*Hydrocotyle ranunculoides*), Fairy fern (*Azolla filiculoides*) and Parrot's feather (*Myriophyllum aquaticum*) can all become too invasive.

Some of these plants are rather pretty, so if you do choose any of them or already have them in a pond, you just need to be aware that your work will be cut out for you keeping them in check, whereas in fact one of the joys of a good wildlife garden, both for the gardener and for the wildlife, is that without invasive colonizers, the pond can generally be left alone.

Some emergent marginal plants such as reeds and sedges can look great at the edge of a pond but can have sharp roots that may pierce the pond liner. Reeds form a dense mat that requires cutting out each year; otherwise it will form great thirsty clumps that will be taking up the pond water to continue growing, so it is worth spending some time looking into the vigour of pond plants before putting them into or around your pond.

CREATING A BOG GARDEN

If it isn't possible to have a pond, or if you would like an additional area next to the pond, you can quite easily create a wetland area of garden, called a marsh or bog garden. This will still be useful to wildlife and is fairly easily achieved. As with making

*The delightful bogbean plant (*Menyanthes trifoliata)
*struggles to survive surrounded completely by the invasive
Canadian pondweed* Elodea Canadensis.

a pond, choose an area which doesn't have
overhanging trees, gets a good amount of sunshine
and is on level ground. Even if you have just made
a pond, this can be a useful way to use up any
leftover pond liner material.

Dig out an area down to a depth of somewhere
between 30 and 60cm, making sure the sides slope
in at a very shallow angle. As with a pond, clear the
area of any sharp stones or other obstructions such
as roots sticking out. Then line the whole area with
pond lining material, calculating it in the same way
as for a pond. For a bog garden, the material doesn't
have to be as good a quality as for the pond itself,
as a few holes will be needed anyway.

Cut a few slits into the area that covers the
deepest part of the hole, so that the plants will have
some drainage. Unlike with a pond, which doesn't
want rich soil, in this case fill the whole area with

*Gayfeather (*Liatris spicata) *is a perennial plant that
thrives in damp conditions and has colourful, late-flowering
spikes of flowers.*

*The yellow iris (*Iris pseudacorus*) makes a striking, early-flowering marginal plant, suitable for any wetland area.*

creatures living in or near it. In the winter, it needs to be mulched over to prevent the area from freezing into a solid mass, which could also destroy aquatic creatures. Ideally a marsh garden succeeds well if there is a way of keeping a trickle of water irrigating it, rather than allowing it to dry out and then get too wet.

The best plants for a bog or marsh garden include many of the marginal plants used at the edges of the pond. Other things worth trying for beautiful flowers are Candelabra Primula. Planted en masse these herbaceous perennials can create a huge riot of colour in a cool, damp corner. If you want a monster-sized plant, try the Prickly Rhubarb, *Gunnera manicata*. It has huge, sharply toothed leaves which can grow up to 2m long so is not for the faint hearted. *Gunnera magellanica* is a smaller sister with a similar style of leaf. Good foliage effect can also be achieved with the Giant Rhubarb *Rheum palmatum* 'Atrosanguineum'; the leaves erupt from buds which seem almost scarlet, then they turn a deep crimson and finally green, before throwing up panicles of pinkish, cerise to red flowers. For a stylish fern, watching the deciduous Royal Fern (*Osmunda regalis*) lazily unfurling its leaves in the spring warmth, before stretching its fronds up about a metre into the air, is a wonderful sight.

If there is no space for a bog garden, or you have no garden at all, it is still possible to create the conditions for bog plants in containers. Simply place a suitable plant in rich soil in an ordinary plant container with drainage holes and then stand this in a larger container which either doesn't have drainage holes or has had the holes stopped up. Providing you keep the larger container well watered, this means the plant will always be standing in water, as it would naturally. This creates an effect that most gardeners have accidentally achieved from time to time when a drainage hole blocks up. A few choice bog plants placed next to each other in this way can be used to great effect in a corner of even the smallest of patios.

a nutrient-rich compost, to just below the level of the surrounding area. Water the area, or allow the elements to do this for you if you are expecting heavy rain and leave the area to settle for about a week before starting to plant.

A wetland garden will require watering in the summer to keep the water levels up and sustain

The huge leaves of Gunnera manicata *unfurling in the spring, add an exotic touch to a bog garden if you have a large enough space to accommodate it.*

CHAPTER 7

Pests, diseases and good companions

Gardening is not just about plants and flowers. Understanding a little bit about the many insects and other mini-beasts that inhabit the garden will help you to recognize what exactly each creature's role is in the greater scheme of things and how to work with, rather than against, the garden's friends and foes.

COMPANION PLANTING

One of the easiest methods of achieving a balance of the good, the bad and the ugly insects in the garden is companion planting. This is particularly popular with vegetable growers and is increasingly seen on allotments but is just as relevant to the home garden, particularly if you are growing some food crops such as fruit and vegetables.

Companion planting, as mentioned in Chapter 3, means putting a secondary, or companion plant, next to the one that you want to protect against pests and diseases. This may work in one of several ways: the companion plant may attract beneficial insects, which will then eat unwanted insects such as aphids from the first plant. Secondly, the companion plant may repel or confuse pests and parasites. A third type of companion planting is called nurse planting, where a plant is grown to provide food for the nearby plant or a handy habitat for beneficial insects. Probably most debatable of the companion methods is the idea of sacrificial or trap companion plants,

Leaving an old tree stump in situ provides a home for beetles and other insects and is not out of place surrounded by the flourishing flowers of a rock rose, (Helianthemum *spp.).*

where a plant is grown to attract a pest and then disposed of, complete with the pest.

Attracting helpful insects

Predatory or parasitic insects tend to have short mouthparts that can't reach far into a flower, to get the nectar and pollen they need. So the types of flowers to grow to attract them tend to have small flowers, which they can reach more easily. Open flowers in the *Umbelliferae* family are particularly

*Leaving cow parsley (*Pastinaca sativa*) to flower in part of the garden will attract many beneficial insects.*

useful. These plants have masses of tiny flowers held in clusters in an umbrella shape. Fennel (*Foeniculum vulgare*), Queen Anne's Lace or Wild Carrot (*Daucus carota*), Cow Parsley (*Pastinaca sativa*) and the attractive 'Toothpick weed' (*Ammi visnaga*) are all in the *Umbelliferae* family.

These plants produce a large amount of nectar, but over a short time, so other plants are required to sustain the insects thoughout the season. It is a good idea to leave the hollow stems of Cow Parsley in place through the winter as they harbour over-wintering ladybirds, which are voracious consumers of aphids.

Many composite flowers are also extremely useful. These are composed of lots of tiny flowers, which make up one composite flower. They produce less nectar compared to umbellifers but many mature slowly, flowering over a longer season. Feverfew, artichoke, chicory, dandelions and many ornamental plants such as calendulas, marigolds, asters and gazanias are in this group and the related Aster family. Sunflowers are a great late addition to the garden, being both good for beneficial insects and providing a mass of seeds for birds as winter draws in.

Pest deterrent plants

The opposite way to work is to protect plants by growing companions that repel some insects. Some carry out both purposes, so dill, for example, repels aphids and spider mites but attracts beneficial insects to an area. Garlic and other members of the Allium family are repellent to a wide variety of insects and garlic and chives are therefore useful for protecting roses from aphids. Planted at the base of a fruit tree, they may deter insects from climbing up it. Basil and tomato go well together both in the kitchen and in the garden: the strong smell of basil will repel aphids and other tomato pests.

*The smell of chives (*Allium schoenoprasum*) and other members of the allium family can repel insects from plants close by that need protection.*

Interplanting

Although we mainly think of companion planting as introducing flowers or herbs, one vegetable can also be interplanted to be a companion for another vegetable. Surrounding carrot plants with onion plants is said to protect carrots from root flies, if there are sufficient numbers of onions. Brassicas will benefit from being planted with alternate rows of another crop. The mixed planting confuses some cabbage pests such as aphids and cabbage root fly.

Whether or not you find companion planting helps, in the kitchen garden it is worth avoiding a monoculture, where you grow rows and rows of the same plant. If you do this, once a pest discovers a suitable plant it will find them every way it turns, so instead of flying off again, it will just move from one plant to the next, quickly devastating the crop. Therefore, wherever possible it is always good to mix plants.

An extension of interplanting is what is sometimes called nurse planting. Native Americans had a planting system called the 'three sisters', in which each plant helped the other to grow. This works with green beans, corn and courgettes or squash. The beans fix nitrogen in the soil, which is then available to help the corn grow. The corn helps the beans by providing support for them as they grow. The courgette or squash leaves shade the soil, preventing weed growth.

Planting a crop such as Nasturtium (*Tropaeolum majus*), which quickly attracts blackfly, might be seen as creating a trap plant. However, this is rather a difficult procedure to get right. The blackfly may be attracted from someone else's garden into yours by the Nasturtium and then move on, before you have had time to dispose of the plant, to a plant you are trying to grow.

Losing the traditional boundaries between fruit and vegetables, as well as adding flowers will help to attract a more balanced range of insects too. As well as adding flowers to the vegetable patch, it is also possible to plant attractive vegetables in flower

A climing bean curls around a sweetcorn plant. This is a form of nurse planting, where the beans fix nitrogen in the soil which is available to the corn, which in turn acts as a support.

beds: vegetables such as Chard 'Bright Lights', which has fantastic foliage with stems in traffic-light colours; or Garlic Chives, which have pretty white flowers on long stems and look just as good as many of the ornamental alliums.

Giving plants the best start, by planting the right plant in the right place, will greatly improve their chances of growing strongly, so they are less likely to get attacked. This means reading the labels on plants, or seeking advice to check that you are choosing plants that suit your conditions. For

example, choose a plant that likes dry conditions for a sunny patch in the garden, or provide damp conditions for plants that like to keep their roots wet. Getting it wrong can mean not only that plants fail, but that they are more likely to suffer from disease. You can often work out how well a plant might grow and how hardy it is by its original provenance. For example, a plant such as *Osteospermum* is native to southern Africa and the Arabian Peninsula. It will therefore prefer the part of the garden that emulates the sunny, dry conditions found there, rather than being consigned to a dark, damp part of the garden.

Companion planting can look very attractive, as a lot of companion plants are pretty and colourful flowers. Even if companion planting doesn't work completely, you are still adding variety to the garden by introducing valuable flowering plants. If companion plants don't fit in with your garden plans, a good general mix of herbs and some annual flowers in amongst the vegetables will still help attract some beneficial insects.

Nasturtium flowers attract blackfly, and can be used as a sacrificial crop to lure flies away from other plants.

If a plant really is overcome with an influx of insects and it seems the good guys are not about to turn up and control them, then in the first instance, you could simply try spraying the plant with a strong spray of water. This will dispose of some types of insects without harming the plant at all. The 'organic' solution many people use is soapy water but not only is it almost impossible to target just one creature without damaging others, it also upsets the balance of nature.

It is difficult to know what damage may be done to creatures by a substance entering the food chain, precisely because the creatures who are affected are wild and we do not always witness the impact chemicals, organic or not, may have on them both in the short and long term. Far better to come to terms with a bit of plant damage and work alongside nature to find solutions. This is a step forward from organic gardening using organic pesticides but is being increasingly recognized as a more sustainable way of viewing how we care for our gardens and the responsibility we have for the wildlife within them.

DEALING WITH DISEASES

Fungal infections

Most plant diseases tend to be fungal and they usually spread and grow from one plant to another with spores, which can be wind-, rain- or soil-borne. Learning to recognize them and to create the conditions where they cannot thrive is all part of gardening in harmony with nature, so that chemical controls become unnecessary.

If you have signs of a fungal or bacterial infection on a plant, then it is important to remove and dispose of the sick plant, although not on the compost heap, as this might harbour the infection. Fungal infections include problems that are commonly seen such as grey mould. The symptoms are that plants develop a fluffy grey mould and rot. This kind of fungus thrives in damp or overcrowded conditions where it can spread rapidly, so allowing plants enough room can help prevent its spread.

In the case of roses, the most common infection is called black spot, which can be bad if the conditions are particularly wet. The leaves become disfigured with black spots, as the name suggests. This brings about the question of plant 'hygiene'. If a plant has a disease, remove all the diseased leaves and infected twigs. In particular, pick them

Roses are very vulnerable to an infection called blackspot, which can be controlled in a variety of ways including choosing cultivars which are less likely to develop it.

all up as they fall on to the soil below in the autumn, as many fungal infections will live in the soil over winter, only to re-emerge and re-infect the plant the following year. So while healthy leaves should be left on the soil, plants with problems need their leaves clearing up. The leaves can't be composted or made into leaf mould, in case they spread the infection.

You could also try putting some repellent companion plants close by. Chives (*Allium schoenoprasum*) may help prevent blackspot on early-flowering roses and garlic, flowering later, may help keep late roses in better health.

The other way forward is to choose varieties that are more infection resistant. Any good nursery will be able to recommend the most resilient varieties and new, more disease-resistant introductions are often advertised.

An infection such as rust, where orange or brownish pustules develop on the leaves, is commonly found on plants such as Hollyhocks (*Alcea rosea*). Knowing which plant is likely to pick up a particular fungus helps in treating the infection. With rust, the spores overwinter on fallen leaf debris, so clean up the area around an infected plant to help prevent this.

Viruses

Viruses are moved from plant to plant by insects such as aphids, or eelworms. Symptoms tend to show as mottling on leaves, malformed growth and

Many gardeners use the technique of companion planting around their food crops, interplanting flowers between vegetables.

reduced crops. Insects are not entirely to blame for viruses, however, as humans can transfer plant viruses, on our hands or on unwashed tools such as secateurs, or by introducing infected plants or cuttings into the garden. Buy certified virus-free plants for certain crops, such as fruit, potatoes and bulbs, or grow plants from seed, so you can ensure you are not introducing viruses with plants like these that are particularly susceptible to them. If you keep getting viruses in one area of a vegetable plot, make sure you rotate the crops each year.

Biological control of pests

Biological controls have been developed mainly because of concerns about using chemicals to eradicate pests. They are predators, parasites, or diseases that are introduced to tackle problems on plants. The predators kill pests, such as aphids. Parasites live off the pest, such as nematodes, which enter into the body of a slug and kill it and reproduce inside it. These are not pleasant introductions. Sometimes a disease will be introduced, such as a

---

FIVE FRIENDLY INSECTS

All of the following insects are useful allies for the wildlife gardener:

Centipedes
Often confused with millipedes, they attack snails, slugs, vine weevils and soil pests, although in times of drought they may lose points by eating plant roots to quench their thirst. Centipedes can be encouraged by providing logs or other decaying wood.

Lacewings
So called because of their large, lacy wings. The adults and the larvae eat their way through aphids, scale insects and caterpillars. As well as providing flowers that attract them with nectar and pollen, you can buy or make chambers called 'lacewing hotels', where they can overwinter.

Ground beetles
A mixed blessing, ground beetles are generally helpful, eating slugs, but unfortunately they share our penchant for strawberries and other fruit. In general, they do more good than harm. A log pile will provide a suitable habitat for them.

Ladybirds
The well-loved ladybird is normally the gardener's friend, eating aphids and scale insects. There are several species, with variable numbers of dots and colouring. Unfortunately, the latest highly-spotted ladybird arrival to Britain is causing havoc, being predatory on the native species. However, the advice at present is not to destroy what one may think may be the predatory ladybird, as it is easy to confuse it with one of the other species. As with lacewings, you can buy or make ladybird boxes where they can overwinter. Don't mistake their ugly

The ladybird manages to eat its way through hundreds of aphids. If you see one on a plant, leave it alone and the plant will soon be clear of aphids again.

larvae for a foe and destroy them; they will be transformed into the pretty ladybird, after they have eaten their way through a few hundred aphids.

Spiders
Unfussy about what might turn up in their webs, spiders will eat flies, woodlice, springtails, wasps and other pests, although sadly helpful insects may also be in their haul. Spiders may thrive around shrubs, or mulches such as straw, so making a suitable environment can encourage them.

bacteria that kills caterpillars without harming other insects.

These kinds of control may well have their place in commercial growing but in a home situation are generally only really effective if used in a contained environment, such as a greenhouse. The timing of their use is critical because if you introduce a predator and there are not enough pests for it to eat, it will die, so getting the balance right is quite difficult. Although we may wish to encourage native insect predators into our garden, biological controls are not introducing native species. Some of the parasites, in particular, also involve introducing insects to a slow and very grisly death, which hardly seems worthwhile when all we might be trying to control are pests on a few ornamental plants.

Introduction of species can go horribly wrong – the cane toad was introduced to Australia in 1935 in an attempt to control the sugar cane beetle on crops there. It has now become a dreadful pest, eating native species and spreading across the country.

LOOKING AFTER THE LITTLE CREATURES

Making a log pile

Even if you insist on having a tidy garden, there is bound to be a dark, dank corner somewhere where you can pile up a few unwanted logs of wood. These will provide a home for a wide variety of insects and a hiding place for several larger creatures.

The logs should ideally be put in a shady spot, so that the wood doesn't dry out too quickly. It may seem strange at first, but decaying wood is vital for wildlife. In the wider world, dead and dying trees naturally provide homes for a wide variety of creatures. Specialized insects then break down the wood so that eventually it returns to replenish the soil.

In the world today, there are substantially fewer places where this is allowed to happen and in our gardens trees are rarely left to decay and die, although it is allowed in well-managed woodland. So to compensate for this and to keep the helpful mini-beasts and other creatures happy, we need to create an artificial area where they can quietly continue their work and continue to survive.

Even if you make leaf mould with cleared leaves, keep some back to add around the woodpile, to help mimic the woodland floor. Decaying leaves provide a home to a variety of invertebrates, and in turn they provide food for larger animals.

Fungi will also live on decaying and dead wood and help it to be re-absorbed into the soil. It also provides another point of interest; identifying the different types of fungi and watching them grow can open up a whole new area. You may even find that you have edible fungi available, although it is best to leave it for the wildlife.

A log pile creates homes for a wide range of insects and can also offer shelter to larger animals in severe weather conditions.

A simple log pile, using wood of slightly varying sizes (over about 10cm in width), can be made by just piling up the timber in a pyramid. If you don't have spare wood in the garden, it isn't difficult to find someone who is cutting down a tree somewhere who can provide the wood, which should still have its bark on it, or you could go to a timber yard. The wood must not have been treated with preservatives and the closer it is to being in its natural state, the better. There are a number of inventive ways in which log piles can also be used to create structures in gardens, too. For example, a log pile held together with a frame of chicken wire and with planks put on top of it can be made into a garden bench, or a pile of logs stacked up together horizontally can be used to create a thick dividing screen in a large garden.

Once you have your log pile in place, resist the temptation to move it around. The rare stag beetle, for example, which breeds in dead wood, has larvae that take six years to pupate, so if the wood is moved around the larvae will probably never make it to become one of these fascinating creatures. A stag beetle is about 7cm long and is so called because its massive jaws look a little like a stag's antlers.

If for some reason you can't create a log pile, another technique to house beetles, that may attract the stag beetle, is to bury a bucket. Take an old plastic bucket and put some holes in the sides of it and bury it up to the brim in the soil, in a quiet corner of the garden. Fill it up with a mixture of woodchips and ordinary garden soil. This will make a good home for several types of insect but do not be tempted to take a peek, as you might disturb pupating larvae. Just enjoy the feeling that you are doing something for the little chaps and every now and then top up the soil as it shifts downwards.

Making a wildlife hotel

Providing insects with a whole range of different materials and sizes of homes can be achieved if you build a 'wildlife hotel'. The easiest way to do this is to stack a few old wooden pallets on top of each other, and stuff a wide range of different hollow objects such as bamboo canes into the sides, along with a variety of materials that different insects might use for nesting. Children particularly enjoy making an insect home, as it appeals to their imagination to think about what might decide to live in there. By making an environment where they can live or breed, many of the helpful, pest-controlling insects will stay in our gardens throughout the year.

A wildlife hotel is great fun to make and can provide a variety of homes for mini-beasts of all shapes and sizes.

THINGS TO PUT IN A WILDLIFE HOTEL

Bits of wood, which will support wood-boring insects and fungi. Include wood with bark, as some small insects live in the spaces between the bark and the wood.

Loose bits of bark, which will attract centipedes, spiders, beetles and the ubiquitous woodlouse as the bark decays.

Hollow stems, such as bamboo canes, or blocks of wood with holes in, for solitary bees to nest in.

Rolled-up corrugated cardboard, put inside a waterproof cylinder and placed in the dry area in the condo might attract lacewings, which eat aphids and other pests.

Hay or straw is useful for some invertebrates, who make hibernation sites by burrowing into it.

THE BUSY BEE

The humble bumble-bee, and other bees, are creatures of major importance not just to the gardener, but to the world. Bees are vital pollinators of many fruit, vegetable and nut crops. A combination of the use of pesticides, the Varroa mite and a loss of habitat, have stressed the health and population of bees for several decades. Now, there is the dramatic new threat of Colony Collapse Disorder, where whole colonies, for reasons we do not yet understand, just abandon their hives and are assumed to have died.

Although there are other creatures, such as some types of birds and other flying insects which pollinate plants, bees are so important to the world that we can all play a role in helping to keep bees healthy and happy.

In our gardens, we can easily help bees in two ways: by providing suitable plants for nectar and pollen from early spring to late autumn and by creating suitable habitats for them. The other most important way we can preserve bees is not to use insecticides in our gardens, as even organic ones can be harmful to them and also break up the food chain that attracts the helpful insects into our garden to maintain a natural balance of pests and predators.

The types of real estate your garden can offer needs to be quite varied, as there are many different types of bees and they require different homes. Some type of bees, such as the solitary bee, tend to nest in the same place for many years, so if you are aware of a place in your garden where this happens, try to leave the area undisturbed.

There can be no sweeter sound in spring than hearing the first bumble-bee flying busily around the garden. Only the mated queen bees survive the winter and so in spring she begins a desperate search for a new home where she can establish a colony. A bumble-bee will nest in the ground or a hedge bank. They are also attracted to old mouse holes and some people believe taking nesting material

*Providing a bee with pollen-rich flowers from early in the year helps their survival. Here a bee enjoys visiting the lungwort (*Pulmonaria longifolia*) which flowers in early spring.*

from old mouse nests and putting them into suitable holes may attract them.

The bumble-bee's natural hedgerow habitat in the countryside has to a large extent disappeared, along with roadside verges and flower-rich meadows, so it is more reliant on an undisturbed area in the garden to nest. Creating artificial homes for them is not particularly successful as they are very fussy about where they nest, but creating suitable general conditions for them will help this increasingly rare species to survive.

Honey bees create much larger colonies, which can contain up to 50,000 individuals. If you have a bee nest somewhere and it really has to be moved, then it is advisable to contact a local bee-keeping group to take the swarm away, rather than getting in a pest controller who will kill them. If there isn't a group close by, a wildlife organization will give advice. Bees are already under major threat, so they do not need humans to deplete their numbers further and it hardly repays them fairly for their vital role as pollinators. Bee-keeping groups are usually great enthusiasts who will be happy to advise on bees in your garden. Of course, bee keeping is a fascinating interest in itself, so with proper advice from a bee-keeping group you could always consider keeping your own hive or two.

In the UK there are around 200 species of wild bees known as 'solitary' bees. Like other types of bees, they are useful pollinators. They are called solitary bees because rather than living in a large hive, they make individual nest cells for their larvae and they don't swarm or build combs like honey bees. Some build these nests in holes in the ground, earth or sand banks, others in crumbling mortar or the hollow stems of plants, or even in holes pre-drilled by wood-boring beetles.

Most wildlife will leave you alone if you leave it alone, including wasps. However, if you feel waspish around them, think twice before you swipe what appears to be an enemy. Several other insects have similar markings to wasps, to ward off predators, but are not stinging insects. Amongst these is the humble hoverfly, a friend of the wildlife gardener. The hoverfly's larvae are keen consumers of aphids and the adults are good pollinators. As a fly, rather than a wasp or bee, it can be distinguished by its short antennae.

A home for solitary bees and other insects can be made quite simply with some hollow bamboo canes.

Solitary bees don't sting and wasps rarely do, but if you stand down-wind in front of their nests, wasps (or bees) may think they are under attack and sting to defend their nests. If you accidentally come upon a nest in the garden, although it may seem counter-intuitive, attempt to stay as still as possible, then back away slowly. If they cease to detect movement, they won't sting. If they are trying to muscle in on your outdoor lunch, distract them by hanging up a jar of jam or similar at the furthest end of the garden away from you.

HOW TO MAKE A BEE BOX

1. Get a bunch of hollow canes, about 1cm in diameter. Some plants such as elder, buddleia or larger raspberry canes are hollow in the centre so these are ideal. Otherwise you can just use ordinary bamboo garden canes cut down to size. A variety of different-sized tunnels may attract mason bees, which then construct cells in each tunnel.

2. Get a sturdy tin or other cylindrical object, such as a piece of drainpipe. Block one end of the tube if both ends are open.

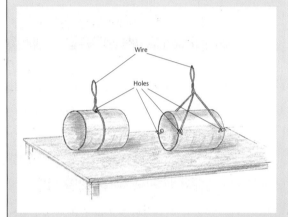

3. Attach some wire or string to the container to create something to hang the container by, either by making a hole in the tin or wrapping the string round it and knotting it.

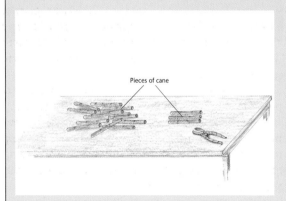

4. Cut down the canes so that they are just slightly smaller in length than the cylinder.

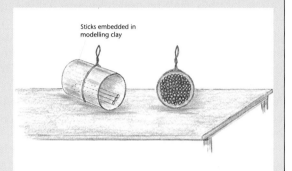

5. Using modelling clay, fix the sticks into the container and keep adding sticks until they are packed in tightly and the container is full.

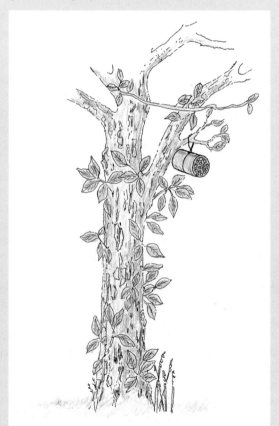

6. Find a location in full sunlight and fix the bee box onto a tree or post, making sure the entrance hangs downwards slightly to keep the interior dry.

Homes for Bees

It is possible to buy ready-made bee houses and tubes especially for bees. However, it is fairly easy to set up your own home. You need a cylinder, some wire, some hollow twigs and some modelling clay.

Another method is to drill a series of holes into a thick piece of wood, up to 20cm in depth. Ideally, it needs to have a bit of an overhang at the top rather like on a bird box, to protect the inhabitants of the holes from rain but any piece of wood or even a log with holes drilled in it and put in a protected place may be helpful. Smooth off any rough edges that may be left after drilling, as these may deter the bees. It can then be fixed to a wall in a sheltered, sunny spot. This method may attract solitary bees, as they nest, as the name suggests, individually. They do not sting or swarm so they are perfectly harmless. When making any home for insects or bees, take care not to use wood that has been chemically treated in any way, since bees may be harmed by chemicals.

As bumble-bees may not readily take to a home provided for them, it is probably best not to invest a huge amount of time and effort into providing homes that they may not use but to concentrate instead on giving them the conditions, such as undisturbed hedgerows, that they might appreciate.

However, it only takes a few minutes to create a home that a bumble-bee might just consider up to scratch, so it is worth trying this simple and cheap idea out. Put some dry leaves into a small terracotta plant pot, then line that with a little bit of moss or feathers. Look for a warm, very sheltered spot, at the foot of a wall, hedge, shrub or tree. Turn the pot upside down, holding on to the material inside as you do this. Wedge a space under one bit of it, which the bees will use to fly in and out. Make sure the pot is secured so that it can't be overturned in wind or by inquisitive animals. Then leave it undisturbed.

Making a nectar bar

One of the best ways to attract bees is to create what is commonly called a nectar bar, which means planting flowers that are all attractive to bees together in one area. The reason for doing this is

Making a nectar bar which includes lots of plants that bees enjoy means they don't have to waste valuable energy searching through unsuitable flower species.

that the bees don't have to waste energy flying around searching for suitable individual plants. Bumble-bees like to feed from one type of flower as they forage, so drifts with groups of the same flowers can be most helpful, especially when they are low-growing plants.

Bees cannot fly easily in wind, so wherever possible put plants for bees in a sheltered and sunny site. Bees need both nectar (as a fuel for flight) and pollen (as a source of protein and fats) to help maintain a colony. As most bee larvae are being raised in the spring, this is the time when they need the most pollen.

Different species of bees will appreciate different shapes of flowers, such as bell, lipped, or tubular flowers and in a mixture of sizes, as the length of the bee's tongue, and how far it can reach, varies from species to species. Some tropical flowers that we now grow have long tubular flowers because they are pollinated by creatures such as humming birds. Bees, particularly bumble-bees, cannot reach the nectar in these long tubes.

Hybridized flowers, which have double rather than single flowers, are not suitable for bees, as the stamens are replaced by extra rows of petals. So it is important when choosing plants throughout the garden to include a good proportion that are from temperate climates, ideally some native species, so that the bees can access the pollen. Bees don't see red, so red flowers are less noticeable to them. For insects generally, orange and yellow flowers tend to be the most popular colours but a range is desirable to attract a variety of species.

When you buy honey, the nectar that the bees have fed on affects the taste of the honey, so certain plants, such as heather, thyme or lavender for example, which appear on the labels of honey, are good indicators of plants that appeal to bees.

Herbs for bees

Many herbs are attractive to bees. Lemon Balm (*Melissa officinalis*) was considered so attractive to them that in *Gerard's Herbal*, it says that in ancient times Lemon Balm was rubbed on the sides of the hives, so that the bees would be able to find their way home. Herbs are useful to humans for many purposes but at the same time helpful for bees, so a herb patch or a few containers with herbs grouped together and within reach of the kitchen door are a great addition to any garden. Many herbs like a sunny, dryish spot in the garden that suits the bees. However, some, such as Mint or Lovage, grow better in a slightly shady, damper position.

ATTRACTING BUTTERFLIES AND MOTHS

Nettles are one of our most useful 'weeds'. For centuries they have been used as nutritious greens, as a herb and were even used to make a stringy sort of cloth. However, for less homespun gardeners, allowing a nettle patch to grow in the garden is an important part of letting the wildlife into your life.

FLOWERS FOR BUTTERFLIES AND BEES

Columbine (*Aquilegia vulgaris*)
Michaelmas Daisy (*Aster novi-belgii*)
Butterfly Bush (*Buddleia davidii*)
Lavender (*Lavandula angustifolia*)
Red Valerian (*Centranthus ruber*)
Globe Thistle (*Echinops ritro*)
Bergamot (*Monarda didyma*)
Evening Primrose (*Oenothera biennis*)
Iceplant (*Sedum spectabile*)

*The lovely columbine (*Aquilegia vulgaris*) will attract both butterflies and bees.*

KITCHEN HERBS FOR BEES

The flowers of all these delicious culinary herbs will also attract bees and butterflies:

Angelica (*Angelica archangelica*)
Chives (*Allium schoenoprasum*)
Fennel (*Foeniculum vulgare*)
Lavender (*Lavandula angustifolia*)
Lemon Balm (*Melissa officinalis*)
Marjoram (*Origanum vulgare*)
Mint (*Mentha* spp.)
Rosemary (*Rosemarinus officinalis*)
Sage (*Salvia* spp.)
Thyme (*Thymus* spp.)
Winter Savory (*Satureja montana*)

Nettles are an extremely important food plant for the caterpillars of some of Britain's prettiest butterflies. The red admiral, the small tortoiseshell, the peacock butterfly all need young nettles, in good sunlight, in order to flourish. They may also attract the painted lady, if no spear thistles are available.

The butterflies lay their eggs in the spring and the new generation will be off by the end of June. After this, it may be an idea to cut back the nettles to stop them seeding too much. This also encourages new growth that may encourage a second flush of tortoiseshells. Once the season is over, nettles can be thrashed down to weaken them before removing a portion of them to prevent rampant overgrowth and self-seeding. The leaves and stalks make a nitrogen-rich addition to the compost bin. If you are tempted to get your own back on the nettle for invasiveness by eating it, use only young growth.

THE GARDEN AT NIGHT

In the evening we may watch the flowers wearily closing their petals and feel the garden is sinking into the apparent stillness of night. Yet, as we sleep, a whole second shift stealthily wakes up in the garden and requires feeding and watering. Nocturnal mammals will waken up around dusk to start their nightly foraging, which may include the many insects that are also most active in the cool of the night. Earwigs, beetles, millipedes, earthworms, woodlice, and slugs and snails are all up and around and munching away, as, in the case of the latter, many a torch-waving gardener has discovered to their horror, as prize plants are demolished without trace before first light.

Amongst the more delightful creatures of the night are the moths. Related to butterflies, they feed on nectar and lay eggs on plants suitable for their larvae, or caterpillars. In the daytime they are frequently camouflaged in hiding places, but on a warm, overcast night, if you put a light on outside, it is surprising what a variety of these creatures can be found in the garden.

Moths are attracted to pale-coloured flowers, as they are more visible at night, and to night-scented flowers. In order to both see the moths and enjoy the night scent of these flowers, it is worth growing them near the house, perhaps under a window so that the scent can waft into the house on balmy evenings.

Some of the larger moths have specific food shrubs and trees which they are named after, such as the privet moth on Privet (*Ligustrum vulgare*); the pine hawk-moth on the Scots Pine (*Pinus sylvestris*); the poplar moth on the Black Poplar (*Populus nigra*) and the lime hawk-moth on the Lime tree (*Tilia cordata*). Several species of moths rely entirely on the Grey Willow (*Salix cinerea*) for food in the spring.

Some moths, such as the herald moth, hibernate as adults in winter in places such as sheds and cellars, so always be careful when cleaning around these areas as they are easily camouflaged.

FLOWERS TO ATTRACT MOTHS

Bladder Campion (*Silene vulgaris*)
Evening Primrose (*Oenothera biennis*)
Honeysuckle (*Lonicera periclymenum*)
Jasmine (*Jasminum officinale*)
Marvel of Peru (*Mirabilis jalapa*)
Night-scented Stock (*Matthiola longipetala* subsp. *bicornis*)
Tobacco Plant (*Nicotiana alata*)
Soapwort (*Saponaria officinalis*)

*Honeysuckle (*Lonicera spp.*) will be enjoyed by many insects during the day but is an important food source for moths at night, too.*

CHAPTER 8

Hedging, walls and trees

THE LOST HEDGEROW

Most of us live in areas where boundaries exist to mark the extent of our gardens. Frequently, these are made with fences or walls. Where possible, by adding or replacing these with hedgerows we will contribute a great deal towards providing habitats that have been wiped out in so many areas. This is mainly due to the changes in farming, where large machinery has resulted in the removal of ancient boundary hedges. As well as providing food and a habitat for many species, hedging also plays a greater role in the ecology of the land, providing corridors of shelter where wildlife can move from one garden to another.

As a result of the loss of hedgerows around farming areas, hedges and the wildlife within it are now dependent on gardeners to give them space to survive. Hedges are great for gardens, offering us areas of privacy, shelter belts, and often providing a buffer against the noise and pollution of road traffic.

When we think of hedging in a garden, we often think of a single species of plant, such as a privet or box hedge. This may be useful for some wildlife, although less so if it is frequently being clipped, as it will not then have a chance to flower. The best kind of hedging involves using a mixture of native species of plants.

*The humble hawthorn (*Crataegeus spp.*) is a native tree that can also be used for hedging. Its fruit provides a feast for wildlife and the blossom lights up a dull corner of the garden in early summer.*

GOOD HEDGING PLANTS

Many of these plants are trees that are tamed into hedging by good formative pruning and then management. On chalky soils, choose Hawthorn, Dogwood, Field Maple, Spindle, Hazel and the Wayfaring Tree. For damp conditions, Willow, Dogwood and the Guelder Rose will thrive.

*Hazel (*Corylus avelanna*) has the advantage of producing nuts which add to its value for wildlife in the hedgerow.*

Dogwood (*Cornus sanguinea*)
Hawthorn (*Crataegus monogyna* or *C. laevigata*)
Wild roses such as the Dog Rose (*Rosa canina*)
Winged Spindle (*Euonymus alata*)
Elder (*Sambucus nigra*)
Holly (*Ilex aquifolium*)
Hazel (*Corylus avellana*)
Field Maple (*Acer campestre*)
Beech (*Fagus sylvatica*)
Hornbeam (*Carpinus betulus*)
Yew (*Taxus baccata*)

Shrubs for flowers and berries

For berries, Firethorn (*Pyracantha* spp.), Barberry (*Berberis* spp.), *Cotoneaster* spp., Buckthorn (*Hippophae rhamnoides*), Blackthorn (*Prunus spinosa*), the Guelder Rose (*Viburnum opulus*) and the Wayfaring Tree (*Viburnum lantana*) can provide flowers, fruit or shelter for wildlife. Wild roses are good for scrambling in amongst hedge plants.

Bees and other insects will love the flowers of *Escallonia langleyensis* and Cotoneasters such as *C. horizontalis*, which hum with activity in the summer and produce plenty of berries and cover for nesting birds. Broom (*Cytisus scoparius*), Flowering Currant (*Ribes sanguineum*), Raspberries (*Rubus idaeus*) and Buddleia are also popular with bees. In the early spring, the first bees will appreciate the delightful *Daphne mezereon* and *Chaenomeles japonica*, the Flowering Quince, which works well trained up a wall.

Creating a shelter belt

One of the important features of hedging is that it can be used to provide shelter from wind in a far more efficient way than a wall or fencing. This helps to shelter both people and plants. Solid barriers buffet wind into turmoil on one side of the wall or fence and then it swirls over the top of the object with added violence, which may damage plants.

Broom (Cytisus scorparius) *will grow on exposed sites and provides a fabulous show of colour with flowers that many insects can feed on.*

Hedging, on the other hand, acts as a filter for wind, slowing it down as it goes through the hedge. It is therefore far more effective as a windbreak.

If you have a windy site, especially a seaside garden, Sea Buckthorn (*Prunus spinosa*), Tamarisk (*Tamarix* spp.) and *Euonymus japonicus* will all stand up to drying winds.

Hedge maintenance

Always check for signs of nesting birds or other animals before carrying out hedge pruning, especially if using mechanical hedge trimmers, as you are less likely to notice this once you get started. Pruning should only be done in late winter as from spring until late summer birds may be nesting in the hedge. If birds have started nesting earlier than usual and before you have had a chance to do the pruning, leave it until late in the following winter. It is anyway better for the plants not to be cut when they are in active growth.

When cutting, taper the hedge inwards slightly so the top of the hedge is a little bit narrower than the base, and light can reach the lower parts of the hedge. Rounding off the edges at the top, rather than cutting straight across the top, also prevents snow accumulating on the top of the hedge, instead making it slide downwards. This prevents the possibility of a heavy fall weighing heavily on the top and breaking branches beneath it.

Daphne mezereon *flowers early in the spring and is therefore a huge bonus for butterflies and bees when sources of nectar are limited.*

A young, native hedge which will eventually grow to create shelter and provide necessary cover for wildlife.

HOW TO PLANT A MIXED WILD HEDGEROW

1. In the autumn, clear the area to be planted to a width of about 60cm. Dig a trench up to 30cm deep.

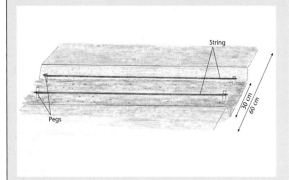

2. Hedging is best planted in two rows. Use some garden line and pegs to mark out two lines about 30cm apart, along which the hedging is to be planted.

3. Soak the plant roots if they have dried out at all, before planting. Use two-year-old bare-root plants of native species, preferably sourced from local stock. Plant along the lines, staggering between the two rows, about 45cm apart.

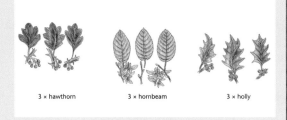

3 × hawthorn   3 × hornbeam   3 × holly

4. Plant three or five of the same species next to each other (depending on the length of the hedge) rather than singly. Then alternate with the next species, planting three or five of these, and so on, repeating the planting pattern in the same order.

5. Backfill with the soil from the trench mixed in with compost or manure. Firm in carefully and mulch the ground with more organic matter about 10cm deep, to help retain moisture and keep the area weed free. Water in well.

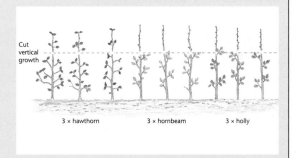

3 × hawthorn   3 × hornbeam   3 × holly

6. In the spring after planting, cut back with secateurs, especially the main growing tips. As many of these hedging plants would normally grow into trees, cutting the strong vertical growth will encourage them to bush out sideways instead. (Yew, Holly, Beech and Hornbeam should not be cut for two years.)

Within about four years the hedge should be well established. Cutting back alternate sides each year may also lessen the impact of pruning. Too much cutting will prevent flowering and fruiting, which is needed for wildlife, so a more informal effect, with less frequent pruning, is more desirable.

GOING UP THE WALL

If you already have established walls in the garden, particularly old or dry stone walls, these can be used to attract wildlife by growing plants within them. The gaps in walls will also provide shelter and habitats for many small creatures, and growing plants in these areas can look very attractive. These plants will often also be useful for filling cracks in paving stones and other areas.

Nature's pretty combination of Corydalis lutea, *Ivy-leaved toadflax* Cymbalaria muralis *and* Campanula poscharskyana *prove that even a dull grey wall can become a thing of beauty.*

Many of these plants are already familiar to us, as we will have seen them colonizing areas. Ivy-leaved Toadflax (*Cymbalaria muralis*) has pretty, delicate leaves and flowers that will decorate the dullest wall. Herb Robert (*Geranium robertianum*) may be seen by some as a weed but has delightful flowers and will grow in quite shady areas.

For the tops of walls, Biting Stonecrop (*Sedum acre*) is a tough, low-growing, succulent plant. Navelwort (*Umbilicus rupestris*) can be spotted growing up the sides of otherwise impenetrable rocks. Its name comes from its fleshy, rounded leaves, which are punctuated by a central belly button. On alkaline soil, the pretty pink flowers of the Maiden Pink (*Dianthus deltoides*) will happily top a wall. The compact pink flowers of Thrift (*Armeria maritima*) sit on a cushion of foliage that clings dizzily on to cliff edges, so it is well suited to enjoying the view atop a wall.

*Pretty in pink; Thrift (*Armeria maritima*) is used to clinging to cliff tops and so works well on top of a wall or in a rocky area of the garden.*

Larger plants, which are better for the base of walls, include the appropriately named Wallflower (*Erysimum cheiri*), Snapdragon (*Antirrhinum majus*) and Red Valerian (*Centranthus ruber*), whose seedlings may need keeping in check to prevent it spreading too far outwards as well as upwards. For damp walls, native ferns will thrive and can make any area look quite magical.

Scramblers and climbers

Growing plants up vertical objects is great for screening unsightly walls, fences and sheds and increases the growing space in a small garden. Many can also be allowed to scramble freely over informal hedging. There are plenty of climbers to choose from which provide fruit, flowers, nesting sites and general cover for wildlife.

Honeysuckle (*Lonicera periclymenum*) will fill the garden with fragrance in the summer and provide nesting sites and berries for birds. Wild Hop (*Humulus lupulus*) is an attractive scrambler that provides food for moths, red admiral and comma caterpillars. White Briony (*Bryonia dioica*) may be considered a weed, but its berries are useful for birds.

Boston Ivy (*Parthenocissus tricuspidata*) or Virginia Creeper (*P. quinquefolia*) can be grown on houses or walls and provides summer foliage shelter for birds and wonderful autumn colour for us. In a shady spot, *Hydrangea petiolaris* will quickly climb and a mature plant will again provide summer shelter for birds.

For fast covering of an area *Clematis montana* will provide the gardener with a flush of pretty flowers; it then quickly creates a tangle of branches, which make suitable nesting sites for blackbirds and thrushes. Clematis can be allowed to grow across other plants, although, like brambles, it will need to be kept in check. Traveller's Joy (*Clematis vitalba*), the wild clematis, provides attractive seed heads that can be left on the plant throughout the winter.

A cultivator of the hop plant, Humulus lupulus *'Aurea', looks very effective twining through roses and has the bonus of providing food for moths and butterflies.*

Take care to cut back plants after they have provided the flowers and fruit the wildlife needs, and not before.

Ivy for wildlife

Ivy (*Hedera helix*) has a special place in the wildlife garden and many uses. It can climb trees, walls or rocks and can also act as excellent ground cover over bare soil and is tolerant of shade, where other plants fail. Walls, fences or other areas covered in ivy are used as nesting sites by several birds, including robins, wrens, chaffinches and blackbirds.

Ivy flowers very late, from September until November, providing pollen for wasps and flies when food starts to become scarce. It offers food for overwintering butterflies, such as peacocks, red admirals, brimstones, commas and small tortoise-shells. Most importantly, the holly blue butterfly has a special need for ivy. It lays its eggs onto the unopened buds of the blossom.

The black ivy berries that appear late into the winter provide food for blackbirds, thrushes and pigeons as they ripen in the spring. Some people believe that ivy will 'strangle' a tree. However, ivy is only able to overcome a tree that is already on its last legs, and rumours of its smothering abilities are greatly exaggerated. It can be kept in check by pruning if necessary and there are many different ivies to choose from, so you could choose a non-climbing, bushy variety. Allowing ivy to grow in the garden will clothe unsightly areas and provide winter greenery as well as providing succour for birds, butterflies and many other creatures.

Planting for a rosy future

While double roses look gorgeous, they are of no benefit to insects and bees, which require single flowers that can produce pollen and nectar. The

Ivy provides shelter and food during the winter, when so many other plants are bare. Here Hedera colchica *'Sulphur Heart' shines through the frost.*

Roses with open flowers such as this one are better for insects and bees who can then access the pollen, whereas double roses are of no use to them, although attractive.

native Sweet Briar Rose (*Rosa eglanteria*), the Dog Rose (*R. canina*), and the tough, disease-resistant *R. rugosa*, with its simple flowers and huge hips, will all benefit wildlife far more than the frilly, fancy confections whose tight petals are impenetrable to insects. This doesn't mean that you need to dig up all your roses, just plant some single roses as well to help wildlife. Scrambling, rambling roses also provide good cover for nesting birds.

Weaving with willow

Willow can be used in an imaginative variety of ways to create living garden structures, from practical fencing to arbours, tunnels or domes, which children will love. The wonderful bending stems are great to weave into all kinds of shapes and supports for plants. If you have the space a simple planting of willow stems can also be regularly

Growing willow can be used to make an attractive natural archway or arbour.

harvested for basket weaving. Willow thrives in soggy soil, so try to place any living structure somewhere damp in the garden, but ideally also sunny. Clear any grass away from the area where the willow will be grown, so it is not competing with this for nutrients from the soil.

Select the type of willows that are suitable for the structure you are going to make. Be sure to find a sustainable source of willow for your weaving. Store the willow in water until it is needed.

TREES FOR WILDLIFE

If you do only one thing to make your garden more wildlife friendly, planting a tree is one of the best. A tree supports a whole host of wildlife. Like most plants, they take in carbon dioxide, a greenhouse gas that adds to climate change. Through photosynthesis, they then release oxygen into the atmosphere. Trees can do this on a larger scale than most plants, and this is why densely forested areas like rainforests, with many very mature trees, are considered to be the lungs of the planet. While one tree alone may not save the planet, every single tree planted contributes oxygen and supports wildlife, flora and fauna.

Trees can block out unsightly views, add privacy and provide shelter from sun, wind and rain in the garden for both you and for your garden wildlife. This is also one way in which we can hope to plant not just for ourselves but for the future too, as many trees will outlive us. Most naturalists would advocate planting native specimens of tree. This means the trees that have been with us since the Ice Age. The flora and fauna attached to these trees have had hundreds of years to evolve and adapt to best exploit the tree.

Introduced species have not had thousands of years to evolve, like native species, and for insects and other creatures to adapt to them. Ideally, trees for planting should also be sourced locally, so that they are best adapted to the local species. It is understandable that if you have your heart set on an introduced ornamental species you may wish to ignore this. Planting almost any tree is better than none, so it is still a good thing to do. It just won't support as much wildlife, so try to find space for a native tree too.

A tree can be planted in a quiet corner or on the boundary of the garden, or made into a focal point in an area of lawn. Remember to check whether a tree you are thinking of choosing prefers acid (ericaceous) or alkali (often chalk) soil, as if it is on the wrong soil type it will not flourish. Many, but not all, conifers prefer acid soils.

Choosing a tree

Some trees can easily be grown from seed but may not always come true to the parent tree, as they may have cross-pollinated with a different variety of the same species. If buying a tree, you can buy a one-year-old seedling, or a whip, which is usually two years old and is the most commonly used size for massed plantings. There are a variety of sizes of more mature, standard trees that can be bought.

A tree can be bought in a container, or bare rooted, or root balled. Containers are useful for trees that cannot cope with root disturbance but the roots may have become pot-bound and will not always establish easily. Some evergreens and larger semi-mature trees in particular are sold as root balled. This means the roots are held together with a fabric or wire mesh. They may well establish better than containerized trees as they are grown in open ground. Buying a bare-rooted tree is the most economic method and they develop a good, spreading root system more quickly when planted. Although it may be tempting to buy a larger tree, a small, bare-rooted one will often take off faster once planted.

Trees establish best if planted in late autumn or early winter. This gives them a chance to establish a good root system before they have to put their energy into putting on top growth. Don't plant in waterlogged soil and avoid poor weather, such as when the ground is freezing or there are high winds.

Once planted, a tree will require regular watering during its first summer and during dry periods in the winter. If necessary, a bit of hosepipe or plastic drainpipe with a cover on it can be planted alongside the rootball, so that water can be poured directly down to the roots.

NATIVE TREES

There are over thirty native trees. When choosing a tree, consider the final height and spread of the tree and whether it is fast or slow growing, so it suits the area of the garden you have in mind.

Here are some of the native trees that you might consider, which all host a good number of insect species or have food benefit for other creatures:

Small-leaved Lime (*Tilia cordata*)
Wild Crab Apple (*Malus sylvestris*)
Wild Cherry (*Prunus avium*)
Alder (*Alnus glutinosa*)
Rowan (*Sorbus aucuparia*)
Whitebeam (*Sorbus aria*)
Wild Service Tree (*Sorbus torminalis*)

Birch, Downy or Silver (*Betula pubescens, B. pendula*)
Hazel (*Corylus avellana*)
White Willow (*Salix alba*) – Goat, Grey and Crack Willow are also good (*Salix caprea, S. cinerea, S. fragilis*)
Holly (*Ilex aquifolium*)
Holm Oak (*Quercus ilex*)
Common Yew (*Taxus baccata*)
Scots Pine (*Pinus sylvestris*)
Black Poplar (*Populus nigra*)

The flowers and fruits of alder are useful to many insect species who benefit where this native tree is planted.

The fine silver bark of birch trees is complemented by a scrambling rose echoing their ghostliness.

Of the native trees, the Pedunculate and Sessile Oak (*Quercus robur* and *Q. petraea* respectively) are renowned as the trees that support the most wildlife. Oaks will eventually mature into large trees, so may not be suitable for a small town garden, especially as it is the mature trees that are the most useful to wildlife. Willow (*Salix* spp.) is probably the second-most useful tree, supporting hundreds of herbivorous species, including many moths, butterflies, bees and wasps. The roots of some willows are notoriously invasive and can cause problems as they seek out water from household pipes. So if you plan to plant willow, make sure it is well away from the house or any drainage pipes. There is a confusing array of willow hybrids but the bay, goat, crack, white, almond and dark-leaved

HOW TO PLANT A TREE

1. Planting methods vary, but the most recent technique that has been proven best for establishing trees is to start by digging a wide, square pit about one spit (a spade's depth) deep. Dig an area at least three times the diameter of the root spread of the tree or the size of the container pot.
2. Add soil improvers if required (depending on the needs of your soil type), going beyond the area of the pit to allow for the eventual spread of the roots.
3. Plant the tree, making sure it is planted at the same level as it was previously planted at the nursery, which can be seen by looking at the soil mark on the trunk. Place a stick across the hole at the planting level to make sure the whole area is even.
4. Drive a stake into the soil at a 45° angle and fix against the trunk with a rubber tree tie and spacer. This will need adjusting as the tree grows.
5. Backfill the soil all around the plant and firm down with your feet so there are no air holes in the soil and to prevent the tree rocking in the wind.
6. Water very thoroughly and then put a mulch over the soil to help retain moisture. Water frequently in the first year.

willows are all particularly good for supporting insects.

Birch trees have attractive winter bark and fine, nervously-fluttering leaves. The two native species are the Downy (*Betula pubescens*) and Silver Birch (*Betula pendula*) but there are also many beautiful cultivars that will still be helpful to wildlife. The male catkins eject little clouds of yellow pollen into the air on a spring wind. It does well on all but very wet soils and hosts over a stunning 200 different insects, including the orange underwing moth. The autumn seeds are attractive to many birds and although it is not a long-lived tree, the trunks of mature specimens make good nesting holes. If you have the space, birch trees look wonderful planted in a group.

The Common Alder (*Alnus glutinosa*) is a slender, fast-growing tree that loves to have its feet dipping into a damp spot, so it is often seen growing by streams and rivers. Its seeds are taken by a number of small birds, and it supports many species of insect.

Native trees under threat

If you don't want a native tree in the garden or the existing trees are not native, it isn't necessary to get out the chainsaw. Most trees will support some wildlife, so just choosing to have trees at all will help some wildlife, even if it is just a place for a bird to perch.

Trees for small spaces

If space is limited, it is still possible to make room for a small tree in a garden and it works well as a focal point and to add structure to an area. If you only have a patio, trees can be grown in containers to great effect. Fruit trees on dwarfing rootstocks will work well and evergreens such as holly, yew or bay look good in a container and can be trimmed into interesting shapes, too.

The Rowan, or Mountain Ash (*Sorbus aucuparia*), doesn't support a huge range of species but is fabulous at providing nectar from its scented flowers; the pretty berries will be enjoyed by birds, while we can enjoy the feast of autumn colour as the leaves change and contrast with the berries. The Rowan doesn't grow beyond 15m and as an added bonus, is said to protect a house from evil.

Hawthorn (*Crateagus monogyna*), which is also used for hedging, makes a wonderful small garden tree and has a fantastic ability to grow in very exposed sites. Sometimes you will see a hawthorn bent double by the wind but surviving nonetheless. Some of the cultivars have pretty double flowers, but as these are sterile (no berries are produced), they are not a good choice for a wildlife garden.

Container-grown trees need to be watered regularly and they will require a little slow-release fertilizer to be added to the compost at the beginning of each season, or to be given a regular liquid feed. Remove about 5cm of compost from the surface and replace it with fresh compost each spring. Every few years, re-pot, teasing out the roots at the bottom, trim any large roots and put the tree into fresh compost and a larger pot if necessary.

*Rowans (*Sorbus *spp.) are ideal trees for small gardens and provide an abundance of flowers, which are good for insects, and then fruit which birds readily take.*

Make sure the pots you use are frost resistant. Plastic pots retain moisture better and are lighter to move around but terracotta pots tend to look prettier. A container will restrict the size a tree can achieve, so it is more suitable for trees that remain relatively compact. A container-grown tree will still sometimes attract a nesting bird and plenty of insects.

Evergreens are very useful for birds in particular, as they provide protection for them in the winter when other trees are bare. There is a wide range of types of coniferous tree such as pine and juniper, which make good garden trees.

Fruit trees to share

Another way to help wildlife in the garden is to include trees that provide flowers and fruit that are of interest to garden visitors. Often we can enjoy the joys of spring blossom, which will help many insects, then with no work on our part, a crop of fruit will appear at the end of the summer, courtesy of those spring bees and other pollinators, adding to both the attractiveness and the usefulness of the tree.

Fruit trees can be bought grown on dwarfing rootstock if size is a problem. Always leave some fruit for the birds, although in the case of cherries in particular, they may well get there before you anyway. Apples, cherries, plums and pears grow readily given the right conditions. It is also interesting to try some of the more unusual fruit trees, perhaps the Mulberry (*Morus nigra*), whose glistening black fruits are popular with birds and badgers. The mulberry's attractive leaves and the gnarled bark of mature trees is quite a sight, although it will eventually grow into a tree that is unsuitable for a small garden. Quince or Medlar trees are always a talking point for an unusual tree and keep these unusual plants going.

A simple Crab Apple tree (*Malus sylvestris*) will act as a host to about ninety different insects, or one of the cultivars such as *Malus* 'John Downie' or 'Red Sentinel' will add spring blossom and pretty fruits in the garden and be nearly as good for attracting wildlife. In late spring, the Wild Cherry (*Prunus avium*), is a good native tree to consider and will attract bees, hoverflies, peacock butterflies and later birds for the fruit. Whatever fruit tree you choose, it is best to adopt the attitude that you share the tree and its fruits with the birds and other creatures. You may feel it is 'your' tree as you planted it, but the wildlife isn't aware of this ownership and take the attitude that it's first come, first served, and that trees – and their fruit – belong to no one.

The woodland floor

If you have an area with several trees, or your garden backs on to trees, the ground beneath it will resemble a woodland floor or border. A shrub layer can be created, which will add some cover for wildlife and be a source of berries and beneath this, in dappled shade, a variety of woodland plants can be grown. It is also possible to create a mini-woodland floor under a single deciduous tree, by surrounding it with a layer of plants kept at shrub height, such as holly and other evergreens, then planting flowers in the shade around that. Many woodland flowers come out in the spring before the tree canopy creates heavier shade.

FLOWERS FOR WOODLAND AREAS

Bluebell (*Hyacinthoides non-scriptus*)
Bugle (*Ajuga reptans*)
Foxglove (*Digitalis purpurea*)
Lords and Ladies (*Arum maculatum*)
Snowdrop (*Galanthus nivalis*)
Solomon's Seal (*Polygonatum multiflorum*)
Red Campion (*Silene dioica*)
Red Dead Nettle (*Lamium purpureum*)
Primrose (*Primula vulgaris*)
Stinking Hellebore (*Helleborus foetidus*)

Foxgloves naturally grow happily on the edge of a woodland and are therefore suitable plants for a shady area of the garden.

CHAPTER 9

Wildflowers, lawns and meadows

WHAT'S THE FUSS ABOUT WILDFLOWERS?

Why bother with native plants? Apart from being a beautiful herald of the seasons, native wildflowers and grasses support insects, which feed birds and many other creatures that prey on them. The growing and flowering cycles of these plants will coincide with the life cycles of native creatures, whereas non-native species may have a different or shorter flowering period.

The disappearance of wildflowers means the disappearance of a large chunk of wildlife. Since the 1940s in the UK, an extraordinary 98 per cent of wildflower meadows have been lost. The causes are building on meadowland, changes in farming practices and the overuse of chemicals. While it may not be possible to emulate the conditions in which wildflowers thrived for centuries, every gardener can grow wildflowers or, even better, create a small meadow area in their garden.

Creating a mini-meadow from seed

A meadow suggests a large area but a small patch of a garden can be used to create this effect and will both look very pretty and benefit wildlife.

Where you live will affect what you should plant. This applies to two aspects of the planting: both the specific conditions in your garden, and more widely, to choosing plants that are native to your area. The plants that are native in a garden next to a Scottish

Cutting a path through long grass and meadow flowers creates an attract effect and the uncut areas provide vital food and shelter for wildlife.

*Growing a few field poppies (*Papaver rhoeas*) is easy to do and will be attractive to bees and many other insects.*

moor are not the same as those that grow on the chalky downs of Sussex, for example.

Native flowering plants can often only survive in a quite local area because the locality also has a suitable pollinating insect. The survival of both the plant and the insect depends on a habitat being provided for the plants. Many cultivated plants have flowers that are unsuitable for the native pollinators.

In the UK, an easy way to find out about the plants that are native to your area is to contact the Natural History Museum, which has a website that lists native plants by postcode. (Details of this website are in the addresses at the back of the book.) Further research will specify meadow plants. Buying wildflower meadow seeds from a reputable source is essential, to prevent seeds being gathered from the wild, which has a negative environmental impact.

It is worth remembering that creating a wildflower meadow should not be just about flowers; it is also about introducing a variety of native grasses, too. Grasshoppers and crickets rely on specific

*Grassland is essential for the survival of our native orchids, such as the Common Spotted orchid (*Dactylorhiza fuchsii*).*

plants and have been particularly threatened by a loss of habitat affecting the availability of these plants. They form an important part of the food chain for other animals. On farmland, carnivorous crickets are also susceptible to pesticides. Grasshoppers feed on grass leaves such as the wonderfully named Crested Dog's Tail (*Cynosurus cristatus*), Red Fescue (*Festuca rubra*) and Cock's Foot (*Dactylis glomerata*). These are all native grasses that should be included in a meadow mix.

It is also possible to buy individual grasses and create your own blend. A grass like Crested Dog's Tail is a great meadow grass and can form about a third of a good grass mix. About a quarter of a mix can be Red Fescue and then the many other grasses, such as Sweet Vernal Grass (*Anthoxanthum odoratum*), or Small Timothy (*Phleum pratense*), can be used in very small quantities of about 5 per cent of the mix.

Types of meadow

The next step is to choose the type of meadow to grow. There is the long-season meadow, or a spring or a summer meadow or a simple cornfield-style meadow.

Cheat's wildflower meadow

If you wish to make a nod towards a wildflower meadow, without getting rid of your present lawn, it is possible to introduce wildflowers into the lawn in plugs, or by over-seeding a lawn. To over-seed a lawn, cut small areas of grass as low to the ground as possible in the autumn. Mix in some wildflower seed with sand and sow over the bare patches, raking the seeds into the ground.

The second method is to grow wildflowers in pots or plugs and transfer them into the ground. If you have a bulb planter, it is worth growing the plugs to fit the size of the hole this will make. Then the bulb planter can be usefully employed to make holes in the turf; these are filled with the plants, which look best clumped together in groups. If you don't have a bulb planter, an old kitchen knife can be used vertically to cut the turf and a long-handled trowel or other suitable tool employed to dig out the holes.

Both of the above methods can be successful but the wildflowers will always be competing with the tough commercial grasses of which most lawns are composed. This means that to keep up a good display of flowers, the lawn may require a similar treatment every few years. It is less likely to be self-sustaining because the finer meadow plants may self-seed but will be competing against fast-growing

Leaving an uncut border at the edge of an area can allow wildflowers to thrive and can be cut back later in the season if necessary.

grasses every spring. However, some shorter plants will succeed and spread, particularly Red Clover (*Trifolium pratense*), which bees love.

If you have the time, some people suggest depleting the soil of nutrients by cutting the grass frequently and removing the clippings for a couple of seasons. This will lower the nutrient content of the soil a little, which will suit the meadow plants. However if you are going to plan that far in advance, it may be worth considering going to the effort of making a self-sustaining meadow.

The self-sustaining meadow

To create a true wildflower meadow area, as stated, the soil needs to be poor and with few nutrients. If you are planting a meadow where there has been a lawn, the soil will be too rich for wildflowers. This is because naturally they are used to surviving in poor soils. If your topsoil is very thin, such as is sometimes the case in chalky or sandy soils, this may not be necessary but if you are planting where there has been a lawn, or you have heavy soil, the top needs to be stripped away completely.

The soil you strip away is valuable and can be used elsewhere in the garden to improve other areas. If it is turf, then you can rot it down by piling it up in squares, grass side down and covering it. When the grass has rotted down it makes excellent, friable soil.

To make the soil even poorer, you can dig in some of the subsoil (the stonier ground beneath the topsoil) with what is left of the topsoil. Doing this is the opposite of what you are trying to achieve everywhere else in the garden, where you are normally improving the soil, but it will help the wildflowers compete more easily for survival.

It is best to start the process by removing the topsoil and digging in subsoil in the winter. Then start off the seedlings early in the spring. (It is possible and in some situations better to sow in autumn but seed may rot on heavy soils, which can get waterlogged.) If you are sowing directly onto the soil, then you will need about 1g of wildflower seeds per square metre, or 5g per square metre for a mix of grass and flowers.

Mix the seeds in with something that will show up where they have fallen, such as sand. This means you will be able to see where the seeds land to ensure even distribution. When you broadcast the seed (which means throwing it down), do so by throwing lengthways and then widthways across each square metre.

Caring for the meadow

If you have created quite a large meadow area, you may want to have a path through it, to enjoy it close-up or for access to other parts of the garden. One of the prettiest ways to do this is to mow a path through the meadow, so the sense of a wild space is maintained throughout the area.

As discussed earlier, bulbs are also useful flowers particularly for early springtime, before most of the wildflowers have taken off, but allow the meadow a year or so to establish before putting in bulbs as well.

Cutting meadow plants

When you cut your meadow grass will depend on whether you intend having a spring, summer or permanent meadow. If you are likely to need a grassy area in the summer, then a spring meadow is the best option. As well as having spring bulbs, this can include Bugle (*Ajuga reptans*), Cowslip (*Primula veris*), Stitchwort (*Stellaria graminea*), Lady's Smock (*Cardamine pratensis*) and Speedwell (*Veronica* spp.). Leave mowing the grass until July, when you can reclaim your recreation area and mow as normal until the next spring.

A meadow that flowers from spring to the autumn will include a mix of spring, summer and biennial plants. Leave cutting it until the autumn, once the seeds have set, then it can be cut right down. Always leave the mowings on the ground for a few days and shake them a bit before removing them, to distribute seed back on to the ground. The dry hay needs to be removed to prevent rot and also to stop adding too many nutrients back into the soil. It can sometimes be used for animal bedding, or put to other good use. For a flush of late summer flowers, mow the meadow in the spring and then in late September.

What flowers succeed best will vary depending on climate and soil conditions and the plants you

HOW TO MAKE A MINI-MEADOW

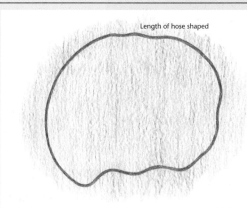

Length of hose shaped

1. Mark out the area to be used, using a piece of hose for a natural line.

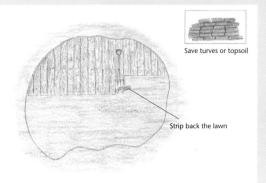

Save turves or topsoil

Strip back the lawn

2. Strip back the area of lawn or topsoil and use elsewhere in the garden.

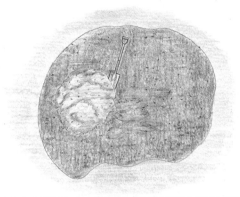

3. Mix some subsoil in with the topsoil and break up any clods on heavy soil.

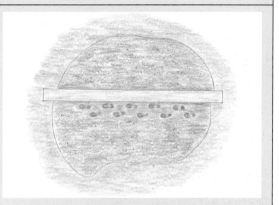

4. Level the ground – a plank can be used for this. Then walk over it gently to compact the soil a little bit.

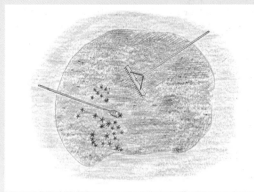

5. In early spring, rake the soil over and leave for a few weeks, so that perennial weeds will start to come up and can be spotted.

6. Remove the weeds and rake the soil again, then broadcast the meadow seed mix over the soil. Cover the seeds very slightly by raking over the soil and protect from birds, with netting or other devices.

*Plants to grow in a spring meadow can include the cowslip (*Primula veris*) which can be mown over in the summer when they have died down.*

TOP TEN WILDFLOWERS FOR A MINI-MEADOW

Bird's-foot Trefoil (*Lotus corniculatus*)
Common Knapweed (*Centaurea nigra*)
Cowslip (*Primula veris*)
Field Scabious (*Knautia arvensis*)
Harebell (*Campanula rotundifolia*)

Lady's Bedstraw (*Galium verum*)
Ox-eye Daisy (*Leucanthemum vulgare*)
Red Clover (*Trifolium pratense*)
Self Heal (*Prunella vulgaris*)
Toadflax (*Linaria vulgaris*)

A mini-meadow can be created in any part of the garden and looks good against a backdrop of foliage plants.

*Self-heal (*Prunella vulgaris*) is often considered a weed in lawns, but it is worth letting it grow and flower through the grass.*

have chosen to grow, so it is always possible to experiment with different planting regimes. If an insufficient number of flowers set seed or you cut down the plants before they have dropped seeds, it is always possible to introduce some plugs with ready-grown plants into any gaps. However, part of the joy of a meadow is that compared to a lawn, once it is up and running, it is quite self-sufficient

and it doesn't require watering, so is much more environmentally friendly.

Traditionally, meadows were cut with a scythe or pitchfork. Scythes are coming back into vogue to some extent but there is a technique to using them well and the blade needs to be kept frighteningly sharp. Strimmers can be used, if you cut the hay down in layers, rather than trying to cut through it all at once. It is also possible to use a long-handled hedge trimmer. With all techniques, the cutting should be done when the meadow is dry.

LOOKING AT LAWNS

In the relative scale of things, a lawn does not support a huge amount of wildlife. However, an open area is good for ground-feeding birds such as blackbirds, which benefit from the worms, and we often like an area of lawn as a place to relax and for children to play safely. Replacing the lawn with a paved area is becoming increasingly common. However, this deprives us all of the wonderful feeling of the grass beneath our feet, and of a childhood of picking daisies and having the smell of fresh grass forever imprinted in our minds.

The more you get interested in wildlife gardening, the less lawn you are likely to want. The celebrity gardener Bob Flowerdew once said that if everyone gave up just a few feet of lawn and expanded their borders a little, the country's wildlife would benefit immensely.

Herb lawns

If you have an area that you are thinking of turfing but will not be walking over a great deal, it may be an idea to consider instead other types of ground cover plants, with a path leading through them. Good ground cover plants will suppress weeds while adding habitat for insects and small creatures, often with the added bonus of flowers. Low-growing herbs such as Thyme, especially *Thymus serpyllum* and Corsican Mint (*Mentha requienii*) can be grown into a carpet and the herbs will be beloved by bees when in flower. More famously, a Camomile lawn can be grown with *Chamaemelum nobile* 'Treneague'. However, a combination of different herbs and plants will offer more diversity for wildlife.

Lawns are not great for the environment in other ways: watering a lawn is a huge waste of water, particularly if tap water is used rather than water from a rainwater butt. Also, as most people now use electric or petrol mowers, keeping a lawn going is using up energy resources. On a sunny weekend

afternoon, the noise pollution created by these machines is unpleasant and often unnecessary.

For small areas of lawn, a manual push mower can do the job more quietly and give a healthy gardener a little light exercise into the bargain. These days there are a few quite light models on the market, or it may be possible to renovate one of the many discarded hand mowers currently doomed to live out their days in the darkest corners of the garden shed.

The turf we use for our lawns tends to contain a mixture of tough grasses that out-compete meadow grasses. This limits the types of insects and butterflies that are supported by it. Yet when you look into grasses, there is a huge range of beautiful species, each attracting different insects and varying in suitability for your own circumstances.

Lawn flowers

Most lawns are cut so close that wildflowers cannot be grown on them. Leaving areas where the grass is cut less frequently will allow a lot of plants to thrive in the lawn and be good for the bees.

Examples of plants that will benefit wildlife in lawns are Clover (*Trifolium* spp.), Violet (*Viola* spp.), Self Heal (*Prunella vulgaris*), Creeping Buttercup (*Ranunculus repens*), Lawn Daisy (*Bellis perennis*), Dandelion (*Taraxacum officinale*) and Common Thyme (*Thymus polytrichus*). Weeds like dandelions and creeping buttercups can become invasive but almost everyone could make room for a few wildflowers in the lawn, even if this just means allowing the daisies to grow and flower, thereby giving the lawn a little sparkle.

Making a lawn wildlife-friendly

If you do not wish to create a wildflower meadow but do want to make your existing lawn more wildlife friendly, there are still a number of ways in which you could achieve this.

One of the first steps to making a lawn into a friendlier habitat for wildlife is to stop using any pesticides, herbicides or fertilizers. Without using weed killers, there are a couple of persistent weeds that may need to be hand-weeded if you do not want them. In particular, dandelion and plantain can be too invasive, or you might just decide to keep them. They tend to be harder to keep under control because they have flat leaves that are left untouched by lawnmowers, so they can grow easily from strength to strength.

The next step is to leave the grass in all or part of the lawn to grow long. The most radical way would be to leave all the lawn to grow. Bumblebees will benefit greatly if all or part of a lawn is left uncut from late June to early August. This is the time when plants like Clover and Birds-foot Trefoil (*Lotus corniculatus*) are flowering. However, there are a variety of choices with cutting lawns. Firstly, it is good to leave it as long as possible before doing the first mowing in spring.

Make sure when you do cut the lawn that the mower is on a high setting so it is not cutting the grass too closely. This way, frogs and other creatures in the grass have a fighting chance of not getting killed or injured. Unfortunately, frogs will quite often freeze when a mower comes towards them, so if the grass is very long, disturb it gently before cutting to try to move animals away. A higher setting above the turf will also give wildflowers a chance to grow.

In a small garden, any area that can be left will still be of benefit, for example leaving grass uncut along a hedge, or around the base of an established tree, or just a quiet, sunny corner with long grass will make a contribution to keeping everything from grasshoppers to seed-eating birds such as finches and sparrows going.

Growing ornamental grasses

In areas of Eurasia and the USA, swathes of grassland are covered in a fantastic range of grasses. If you have no lawn, another way of introducing

Introducing ornamental grasses into the garden can create dramatic effects. The birds eat the seeds and insects can find winter homes in the stems.

grasses and seeds for birds into the garden is to grow ornamental grasses in a mixed border. These grasses may not all be native but as well as providing seeds, they can be left standing in winter giving the garden architectural interest while providing homes for insects in their stems. The American prairies provide a fantastic example of some of the giants of the grass world.

Bringing in bulbs

Whether or not you decide to introduce wildflowers into your lawn, or cut back on the mowing, an easy way to add colour and create a bit of variety into the grass is to plant bulbs. The flowers will be useful to insects, especially the early spring bulbs.

Daffodils are probably the most popular choice for adding sunny cheer at the end of a long winter. Choose the size of daffodil depending on the size of the lawn. A small area looks better with smaller plants, and early-flowering varieties such as *Narcissi* 'February Gold' or 'Tête à tête' will put on a big splash of colour without getting too large. Although it is tempting to buy a big mixed sack of daffodils, they always look better if they are restricted to swathes of the same type.

To get a natural effect, scatter the bulbs on the ground first, so that they are placed randomly. If

Putting daffodils in a lawn is an easy way to add spring colour and help out insects searching for food in the spring.

you are planting a lot of bulbs, a bulb planter tool can be useful. This removes a plug of soil and the bulb can be planted beneath it and the plug replaced. A swathe of bulbs generally tends to look more effective in a sunny corner rather than creating an island in the middle of a lawn.

The leaves of bulbs need to be left for at least six weeks after flowering, so the bulbs can store enough energy in their roots for the following year. There is no need to tie the plants up as this only restricts this process. This is a good reason for choosing early-flowering bulbs, as you need to allow this time before mowing a lawn.

Once the bulbs are in, they require little care and will reward you with colour every year. Crocus will naturalize and the fine leaves soon blend in with the grass as they die back. *Fritillaria meleagris*, the Snake's Head Fritillary, is a wonderful choice if you have a damp, slightly shady area of grass. Many other bulbs can be grown in lawns, such as *Allium moly*, *Anemone blanda* and the Spring Snowflake *Leucojum vernum* var. *vagneri*, which starts to flower in late winter. Meadow Saffron (*Colchicum autumnale*) will grow happily through grass, giving a lovely flush of colour, as the name suggests, in the autumn.

*The delightful Snake's-head fritillary (*Fritillaria meleagris*) will grow through grass and naturalize in a damp area.*

CHAPTER 10

The bigger picture

Once we look into gardening for wildlife, it becomes impossible not to consider the wider impact our gardening has on life in general in the world. We know that every action we take affects the planet in some way or other but gardening, which can seem like quite a benign activity, can also impact negatively on the planet so it is important for us to consider what we can do to make sure it is the wonderful, life-giving force for good that it can be.

The terms 'eco-gardening' or 'sustainable gardening' are increasingly being used to explain this new style of gardening. Gardening organically is to some extent a given, when gardening for wildlife. But gardening in a way that is sustainable by the planet and doesn't create a heavy carbon footprint is a step further in the right direction.

Areas that need to be addressed when we consider this include ceasing to use non-renewable resources in gardening, using water wisely, keeping seeds in public ownership and the creative use of ground in urban spaces, which may help to prevent disasters such as flooding.

Even the simplest of things require a little thought. If you buy, for example, a tree fern for your garden, it has already notched up a considerable carbon footprint by the fuel used to transport it from a country such as New Zealand. This journey will have had an impact on global warming, as fuel will have been burnt to transport the plant. Of course, it also needs to come from a reputable source, as imports of plants which are denuding native wildlife elsewhere are unacceptable and often illegal.

A grass roof is used to help camouflage an unattractive building and blend it into its surroundings.

So when planting a garden, it is worth considering what ecological costs have been involved before it arrives in the garden centre or nursery. This may include pollution involved in the mechanization of growing plants, or growing them out of season in greenhouses when we can grow them in season without requiring additional heat or light, or other growing techniques that are not sustainable.

RECYCLED GARDENING

One of the simplest things that we now need to consider is what to do with all the plastic pots that plants are sold in. This has been described as the plastic bag problem of the gardener's world. At the moment, as long as most pots are not made of biodegradable materials, we need to be sure to recycle them rather than binning them. Some garden centres are trying out having recycling bins for pots, so that is one option.

Most gardeners seem to find at some point that they are getting buried under a sea of plastic pots. However, there are often gardening groups who would welcome them, such as charity or school gardening groups. Otherwise, it is worth joining an organization such as Freecycle (www.freecycle.org), where you can advertise the pots and local people who need them will come and collect them.

Organizations such as Freecycle are also useful for disposing of unwanted tools, topsoil, hardcore, old greenhouses and sheds. Old tools are also welcomed by other charities and some allotment groups will recycle them too.

At the garden centre, another consideration when buying articles of garden furniture and other wooden items, is to check that the wood itself comes

Acquiring plants that are often grown locally such as this Centaurea montana *cuts down on the ecological impact of gardening.*

Plastic pots are having a troublesome impact on green gardening; recycling them is essential.

from a renewable resource. Approved wood is always labelled as such and it is best to only buy from retailers who belong to a certification scheme, such as that run by the Forestry Stewardship Council (FSC).

To source wood for making raised beds or other garden items, you can also lower the impact of this by finding a local wood recycling project to source the wood. A garden or an allotment is also a great place to recycle unwanted objects in creative ways. Next time you are taking an item to the dump, it is worth considering if you could make it into a planter or, in the case of old sinks and baths, even a pond.

The peat and moss problem

One of the most controversial ways in which we denude our land, or the land of other countries, is by buying compost that contains peat. The chances are, if a bag of compost doesn't say it is peat-free, then it contains some of this non-renewable resource.

This peat comes from bogs, which have shrunk massively because of the demand for it in compost. This means a whole plethora of wildlife that has survived in this special habitat, such as unique insects and mosses, are greatly endangered as a

Finding creative ways to recycle unwanted objects can be fun and make a talking point.

result of this. Even if a bag of compost includes peat that is not local, it will have come from another country, costing them habitats that have supported wildlife for thousands of years.

There is little point in boosting your wildlife garden soil with peat at the expense of the wildlife of a peat bog. Nowadays, there are an increasing number of peat substitutes, so when buying any kind of compost, check that it is peat free. Some biodegradable seedling pots are also made of peat, but again there is no reason to use them, as there are alternatives now available.

Sphagnum moss is also under threat. Moss may seem to just be a lawn weed but this particular moss is home to a vast array of insects that cannot survive elsewhere. Sphagnum moss was used in hanging

Moss is sometimes used as a lining for hanging baskets but it is a valuable resource for insects and so it is better to replace its use with other more sustainable materials.

baskets or to make decorative wreaths but neither is necessary these days as there are plenty of substitutes on the market. It is also possible to change the style and way in which you make up your hanging basket or wreath, to eliminate the usage of moss.

These two non-renewable resources are still on sale in many garden centres. It is important to remember that just because some places are willing to sell them it doesn't make it okay to buy them. The further consumer demand falls, the more time and resources will be spent developing alternatives in this lucrative market.

It is also always worth considering the carbon footprint involved in bringing a product to the garden centre in terms of transportation. With peat-free compost, for example, there may well be a more local, cheap option of buying various types of compost or soil conditioners from farmers or the local council green waste recycling plant. This is often cheaper for bulk amounts of soil anyway.

Better still, make your garden more eco-friendly by making as much of your own compost as possible, so that your green waste is being recycled and providing you with the best compost you could hope for. It is also free.

USING WATER WISELY

We are becoming increasingly aware that water is a priceless and precious commodity. When there have been summers with drought, this hits the gardener hard, both in terms of hosepipe bans and the cost of using tap water for essential watering.

It is becoming clear that our water use needs to change. Suddenly we are beginning to realize how absurd it is that water that has gone through a highly complex system to provide us with clean drinking water is the same water we use to flush the toilet or water the plants. This processing is in itself a huge waste of energy, as our plants would much prefer rainwater anyway.

Fitting one or two water butts either to the guttering on the side of a building, or, on an allotment or in the garden, onto the shed or greenhouse, provides a good supply of rainwater, which is free and would otherwise be wasted. It is extremely simple to fit butts and they are now available in quite a few different styles and materials; the traditional plastic one is not the only choice.

A simple water-saving idea in the home is to put a bucket under the tap in the shower or bath, if the boiler is the type that takes a minute or two for the hot water to come through. This usually gives almost a bucket of clean, fresh water that can be used on the garden. Some people are also trying out pumps that drain grey water out of the bath, although they require filters to prevent too much soap getting on to the ground.

It is also possible to fit a kit that diverts grey water from a down-pipe. This should only be done on a bath or shower pipe, as kitchen sink water tends to contain grease and chemicals. Although grey water contains some soap or shampoo, this tends to be heavily diluted. It may also make you reconsider how much soap you actually need to use, as we tend to add an unnecessary amount to our water systems anyway.

Grey pipes can also be attached to washing machines; however, it is then necessary to use low-sodium detergents in this case, as sodium will damage the plants and soil. Phosphorus in detergents should also be avoided as it can cause algae blooms on ponds or waterways.

Around the plants themselves, the most effective way to retain water is to make sure the earth has up to four inches of mulch on top of it. This means

A water butt can easily be attached to guttering on a shed, to provide easily accessible water for the garden.

any kind of compost or bark chippings, or even ground cover material. The mulch acts as a barrier and keeps the soil underneath it warm, but also moist. If you dig down into a soil that has been properly mulched, the top of the ground can seem deceptively dry but below the soil is still moist. Be careful not to put the mulch too close to young plants though, as the nutrients in it can 'burn' the plants.

The design and position of planting beds may also affect how much moisture they will retain, so it is worth considering this too. For successful gardening, choosing the right plants to cope with the conditions is vital. Rather than being stuck trying to keep a water-loving plant going in a hot, sunny border, try making sure that water lovers grow only in damp areas and choose more drought-resistant plants for drier spots.

MAKING ROOM FOR WILDLIFE

One of the biggest problems our wildlife faces is the ever-decreasing space it has in which to survive. One of the ways to help wildlife in the garden is to look at how we can create more green spaces.

The parking problem

We all know the problems that can arise in some areas due to lack of parking space but we need to also consider the impact this is having. The trend

This eco-house, nestling amongst older buildings, was designed to include a sedum roof, a water butt and many other sustainable features.

in recent years for paving over front gardens is beginning to be questioned, as it can cause localized problems during flooding. With so many people paving over front gardens there have not been enough areas of soil for water run-off, overloading drainage. This can have a devastating effect on wildlife in a wider context, because as well as localized flooding, excess sewage can end up being pumped into rivers because of overloading, which damages river wildlife in a major way.

Ground drying beneath extensive paving can also increase the risk of house subsidence. Choosing permeable materials will help prevent this. We also need to seriously consider whether such large areas really require paving.

It is also possible to keep the front area of a property green and permeable by parking on grass that has been overlaid with a durable honeycomb structure, like an open mat, made out of concrete or a hard type of plastic. Some people also leave strips of soil in the area between the car's wheels. In this sort of area, or on gravel, drought-tolerant plants will fare well, including thymes, which will give off a fantastic aroma if your parking is a little askew.

While off-road parking may be required in what was once a front garden, it is quite possible to redesign an existing or new parking area to build in trees, shrubs, raised beds or even just pots to 'green' up these areas. There are often spaces around an existing parking place, such as next to a fence or wall, which can be utilized by the creative gardener, with climbing plants and possibly hedging. All these will be a great help in absorbing excess rainwater.

Legislation has been introduced to make paving over gardens something that will soon require more thought. In England, planning permission is required if you intend to use impermeable materials such as asphalt to cover a front garden. These measures have been taken to try to encourage the public to consider what materials they use in converting front gardens, and may also perhaps help people to appreciate the importance of considering whether it is really necessary to remove a front garden. Over 50 per cent of front gardens have so far been lost to parking, so every garden kept (or with parking paving minimized, and the rest of the front garden greened up) is a step in the right direction.

*On a small, dry, gravel area, a covering of houseleeks (*Sempervivens spp.*) can look great.*

LIVING ROOFS

One of the easiest ways to add an area to your garden, which will contribute to wildlife and will be a great talking point, is to put a living roof on a building. Living roofs attract a wide range of invertebrates. Shield bugs, ladybirds, hoverflies, butterflies, bees and grasshoppers will take advantage of the habitat. More unusual species such as squash bugs and leafhoppers, which enjoy warmer temperatures, may be attracted to the rocky, Mediterranean-type landscape they find on a living roof.

Creatures such as predatory beetles like burrowing among loose, dry soil and around plant roots, and a variety of bees and wasps will live in or visit the area. Butterflies and moths will be attracted to a wildflower roof containing vetches and Bird's-foot Trefoil flowers on which they can feed, and they will like the dry conditions with areas of bare shingle or gravel.

Seed-eating birds such as the chaffinch, linnet, goldfinch and greenfinch will be attracted to the roof providing seed heads are left for them and blackbirds, song thrushes, robins and wrens will enjoy grubbing around on a roof.

In the garden, creating a living roof can be quite simply done on the roof of a shed or summerhouse if it isn't too steep. As well as the benefits to wildlife, a green roof on a shed is often easier on the eye than the standard bitumen roof that most sheds have and helps the building blend much more successfully into the surrounding garden.

Next to the house, garage roofs can also sometimes be incredibly ugly and adding a living roof can greatly increase the habitat area for all kinds of creatures and make the area into an attractive feature. A living roof may even offer some additional protection and leak prevention to the original roof, stopping the ageing effect that the sun and frosts can have on waterproofing materials used on roofs.

Wherever you choose to add a living roof, do check carefully that the building will be able to take the additional weight and if you are uncertain, get in one of the organizations that are used to building

Sedums are particularly good plants for green roofs. They are drought tolerant and very tough and add colour and texture to the area.

them for you. Once the roof is up, remember to check the structure is still sound after heavy storms and winds. Extra weight can put a strain on the windows in a shed or summerhouse, so check they are properly supported and if necessary add additional supports inside the building.

The two planting types for living roofs appropriate in a domestic situation are called shallow (or extensive) and deep-rooted (or semi-extensive) systems. Which type you choose depends on the depth of growing medium you wish to have and the plants that can survive in it, and also what kind and how much maintenance each type requires.

A shallow roof is the most common type, particularly for an area like a shed or garage. This is the lightest type of living roof and the soil (or substrate mixture especially for a roof) can be any depth between about 20 and 100mm. However, the types of vegetation it supports will be limited to plants such as sedums, because it is necessary for the vegetation to be very tough and drought tolerant. On a roof, a plant is also continuously exposed to winds and frost. An idea of the kinds of plants that might suit a roof garden are those that thrive wild in coastal, cliff or mountain areas.

A sedum roof is pretty drought tolerant, although a very severe lack of rainfall might lead to some patchiness where plants have died back. However, this in itself is not a bad thing, as it may provide an environment in which some birds enjoy scratching around for insects. Added to this, it is also possible to buy ready-made sedum roofs from some suppliers, which can be rolled out so that they are up and running immediately. In shady, wetter areas, it is possible to create interesting effects with mosses.

The depth of actual substrate required for a sedum roof is up to 5cm in depth but if you wish to go for deeper planting, you need to double that. With up to 10cm of substrate you can grow wildflower meadow plants. These will include low-growing perennials such as small bulbs, alpines and grasses. The larger the diversity of plants, the longer the flowering season so more insects can collect nectar throughout the flowering period.

A deeper style of roof planting, called a semi-extensive roof, has a greater substrate layer, between 10 and 20cm deep. With this depth of soil, which is only suitable for a reinforced roof, a wider diversity of plants can be grown, creating a mini wildflower meadow, using bulbs, grasses, and dry habitat annuals and sub-shrubs. This diversity can create a naturalistic planting but will require a little maintenance, as it will need weeding to keep the diversity going.

Tree seedlings also need to be removed, as their roots could break down into the building's roof and affect the waterproofing. With wildflower roofs, these can be cut towards the end of the year and the clippings left on the roof for birds. If the roof becomes too thatched with clippings, these can be removed towards the end of the winter.

In commercial settings such as on the top of office blocks, there are now some excellent examples of intensive, very deep, living roofs. These in effect are gardens on top of buildings and require serious structural thought before being embarked upon but when new buildings are being considered which take away land, green areas can always be considered as a way of utilizing space that is otherwise removed from wildlife.

First, the roof needs to be fully waterproofed. A frame is then put on top of the roof, which will prevent it from slipping and hold in the soil and grit. On larger roofs, a drainage layer is then put on, so that excess water can run off. Conversely, the next stage is to add a layer of material that will retain moisture, to keep the plants happy, as they will be getting both a baking and lose moisture from wind on a roof. This can be something as simple as old towels, or if you are buying in the roof garden plants, they may come with this layer attached.

Finally, the substrate is added and the plants put in, either in the form of a pre-grown sedum blanket, which can be rolled out, or even matting that has been impregnated with wild flowers. The home-made way is to have plug plants ready. This means small plugs of wildflowers, or cuttings of sedum, which are manually planted across the substrate. This is far more work but cheaper than buying ready-made blankets and with wildflowers it means you can use species which are specific to your locality.

It is also possible to sow seed on the area but there can be difficulties with the seeds getting blown or washed off before the roof is established. Faster growing weeds may also take advantage of the bare

With space for wildlife becoming more limited, extra areas such as green roofs are becoming more essential for their survival.

MAKING A LIVING SHED ROOF

There are several different ways of making a light living roof. Here is a suggestion for a simple method, suitable for a shed:

1. Put a layer of a waterproof membrane, such as butyl pond liner or 300-micron damp proofing polythene, onto the roof, ideally in one continuous sheet, and nail it down.

2. Add some layers of fleece matting. This can be anything from old blankets or towels, which will help the substrate retain moisture.

3. Measure up and create a wooden frame from recycled wood, which can be nailed down on top of the roof.

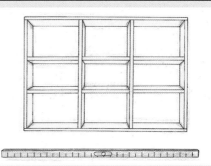

4. Put down a layer of a light material for drainage, such as clay granules, mixed with a layer of substrate of crushed brick, limestone chippings, grit or shingle, mixed with some subsoil.

5. Plant up and water very thoroughly, checking inside and out for any drainage problems.

soil. If sowing seed, mix it with sand to help get an even spread across the area. Planting plugs or seeds is best done in the autumn or spring, when some rainfall is expected. The summer is the least suitable time to plant because there may be periods of drought, drying the plants out before they have had a chance to get established.

When choosing sedum plants, the native sedum is Biting Stonecrop (*Sedum acre*), which can often be found on old walls, rocks and some roof areas. The most commonly used species for roofs, however, are *Sedum album*, *S. hispanicum* and *S. reflexum*. White and Biting Stonecrop have the best flowers for attracting butterflies, bees and other insects.

A green roof can be made fairly simply, and in fact on an industrial scale, living roofs can provide insulation, cooling, and by absorbing rainwater prevent flash floods in drainage systems.

It is also possible to create a green roof or a small alpine garden on an area that houses recycling or rubbish bins. Apart from making an otherwise dull area more attractive, you can enjoy watching the plants growing every time you take the rubbish out.

GOING ORGANIC

I advocate using no chemicals at all in the garden, on the basis that almost all problems right themselves when the environment is well balanced and the gardener nips problems in the bud. Understanding what problems there are and how to solve them without resorting to chemicals is the key to successful gardening. It is often the novice gardener who most often reaches for a chemical solution to a problem, often without even knowing if they have identified the pest or disease correctly.

If you do choose to use chemicals, it is better to familiarize yourself with the organic options. However, it must be emphasized that because a solution is organic, this does not in any way mean it is harmless. A simple solution of soap put on to aphids, for example, will clog up their pores and kill them. This is an organic method. However, it will also kill the 'good' predators on the aphids, so you will be doing more harm than good, as you will be disposing of nature's pest controllers. Bees are particularly at risk from the use of chemicals.

Have a little patience, and birds and predatory insects will do the job for you. So before using any organic pesticides, it is worth educating yourself about how they actually work and whether or not they may also have a negative impact on food sources for wildlife in your garden.

Just because a garden centre or supermarket sells pesticides, it doesn't mean that a responsible gardener should use them on the garden. Sometimes people will say that a product must be okay if it is allowed on the shelves but sadly there are often latent and long-term problems with chemicals which are not always addressed. Shops and their suppliers in particular are working to make a profit, not to save wildlife.

When it comes to herbicides (weed killers), some gardeners argue that they cannot keep on top of the

Bees are particularly at risk from the effects of pesticides used on other insects.

The wildlife gardener can see the beauty and usefulness of plants that are often dismissed as weeds.

and hoes, there is a very human solution. If you can afford to do so, employing a gardener to do tasks that have become difficult can give a whole new lease of life to an overwhelming garden. It costs the planet nothing and means that a younger generation of gardeners can find work.

Make sure the gardener you choose understands the concept of gardening with wildlife in mind and is not about to nuke your garden with chemicals. Any good organic gardener will understand this, and there are plenty of them in need of work. There are also volunteer schemes for people to lend a helping hand in the gardens of the elderly or infirm. So if weeding is a worry, it is worth considering some human help before reaching for herbicides, whose long-term effects we cannot know.

The more you garden for wildlife and relax a little about what you allow to grow there and who or what hangs out in it, the more you can see how diversity attracts a wide range of creatures that will keep your garden and its plants in the best of health.

SUSTAINABLE LIVING

It's good to have an area in a wildlife garden that is to provide food for you, not just for wildlife. There is nothing as satisfying as having some fruit or vegetables fresh from the garden and it means that the small amount that you are growing rather than buying cuts out all the air miles bought food creates and brings you food that you know is absolutely fresh and chemical free.

Growing some crops doesn't have to be a full-scale activity but a few packets of seeds can go a long way to making fresh summer salads, or so many other things that can be grown. If you don't feel you have time for gardening, just adding perennial food plants, or fruit trees and shrubs will give you fruit every year with very little effort on your part and if you don't get around to eating it, the birds will appreciate them too.

Seedy stuff

Another area of sustainable gardening that is well worth giving some thought to is seed saving. Since 1964, all varieties of vegetable seeds have had to be

garden without the use of chemicals. While there is a new generation of weed killers that work by systemically killing the plant, from the top to the roots, there are still problems with these, in that there is some discussion about whether the surfactants that make the chemical stick to the plant could be harmful to the environment.

However, the best non-chemical weed killer is a pair of strong hands. If you are unable to spend the time or physically less able to remove weeds by hand

To cut down carbon emissions, try growing some of your own crops, such as these sweetcorn seedlings grown in old toilet roll tubes.

registered under the Plant and Seed Act. Registering seeds is expensive and as a result of this, seeds mainly get registered when they are grown for commercial harvesting and crop heavily and store and travel well. However there are many, many varieties of seed which may not have all those attributes but which nonetheless can have a fantastic taste and are part of our national heritage. Many nurseries that stocked more unusual seeds could not afford to register them and so they started to go out of circulation.

Fortunately, there are a couple of organizations that are helping to save seeds so that these varieties will not be lost. The first is the Heritage Seed Library (part of Garden Organic). It works to collect and therefore save seeds from vegetable varieties at risk of dying out, and distributes them to its members to grow, enjoy and save further seeds for the future.

The second group of organizations are the seed-swapping groups, such as Seedy Sunday (www. seedysunday.org). They function by encouraging people to swap seeds, rather than buy and sell them. This means that they bypass the law that means only registered seeds can be sold and also make obtaining seeds a sustainable activity, so that people will consider doing this rather than always buying packets of new seeds. Seed swapping may help contribute to bio-diversity, which in turn is good for wildlife. Going to a seed swap is also a great place to meet like-minded people, sharing information about sustainable gardening.

Whatever you choose to do with your garden, getting into growing in a way that means you and your plants will be encouraging wildlife into your garden is sure to set you on a path to enjoying the huge benefits of gardening in harmony with nature. As well as the great pleasure this brings as the wildlife slowly creeps into your world, it means you will also be gardening in a way that will sustain life in your garden – not just for now, but for future generations, too.

TEN WAYS TO A BETTER FUTURE

Turn a flat root into a green roof.
Make a nectar bar for butterflies and bees.
Plant a native tree.
Make a pond, no matter how small.
Compost kitchen and garden waste.
Change fencing into hedging.
Change a lawn into a meadow.
Make some homes for mini-beasts.
Control pests and diseases without chemicals.
Grow some food crops in your garden.

Bibliography

Buczacki, Stefan *Collins Wildlife Gardener* (HarperCollins, 2007)

Chinery, Michael *Attracting Wildlife to Your Garden* (HarperCollins, 2004)

Chinery, Michael *Garden Wildlife of Britain and Europe* (HarperCollins, 1997)

Dunnett, Nigel and Kingsbury, Noel, *Planting Green Roofs and Living Walls* (Timber Press, 2004)

Huntington, Lucy *The Wild Garden* (Cassell, 2000)

Mabey, Richard *Flora Britannica* (Sinclair-Stevenson, 1996)

Packham, Chris *Creating Your Own Back Garden Nature Reserve* (Bookmart, 2003)

Royal Horticultural Society and Royal Society of Wildlife Trusts *Birds in Your Garden* (Think Books, 2007)

Royal Horticultural Society and Royal Society of Wildlife Trusts *Wildlife Gardening for Everyone* (Think Books, 2006)

Ryrie, Charlie *Wildlife Gardening* (Cassell, 2003)

Stevenson, Violet *The Wild Garden* (Frances Lincoln, 1998)

Thompson, Ken *No Nettles Required* (Eden Project Books, 2006)

Walters, Martin *Gardens for Wildlife* (Aura Books, 2007)

Wilson, Matthew, Royal Horticultural Society, *New Gardening* (Mitchell Beazley, 2007)

WEBSITES

BBC
www.bbc.co.uk/breathingspaces
www.bbc.co.uk/gardening

Butterfly Conservation
www.butterfly-conservation.org

Freecycle recycling organization
www.freecycle.org

Heritage Seed Library
Garden Organic (Henry Doubleday Research Association)
www.gardenorganic.org.uk
www.livingroofs.org

National Hedgelaying Society
www.hedgelaying.org.uk

National Society for Allotment and Leisure Gardeners
www.nsalg.org.uk

Plants by Postcode – Natural History Museum
www.nhm.ac.uk

RHS in partnership with the Wildlife Trusts
www.wildaboutgardens.org

www.seedysunday.org
www.seedswap.org

The Soil Association
www.soilassociation.org.uk
www.thegreenroofcentre.co.uk

Woodland Trust
www.woodland-trust.org.uk

Further information

USEFUL ADDRESSES

Bat Conservation Trust
Unit 2, Cloisters House, 8 Battersea Park Road,
London SW8 4BG
020 7627 2629
bat helpline 0845 1300 228
www.bats.org.uk

Buglife
The Invertebrate Conservation Trust
170a Park Road, Peterborough PE1 2UF
01733 201 210
www.buglife.org.uk

Bumblebee Conservation Trust
School of Biological and Environmental Sciences
University of Stirling, Stirling FK9 4LA
www.bumblebeeconservationtrust.co.uk

Froglife
9 Swan Court, Cygnet Park, Hampton,
Peterborough PE7 8GX
www.froglife.org
01733 558960

Flora Locale
Denford Manor, Hungerford, Berkshire RG17 OUN
01488 680 457
www.floralocale.org

Fauna and Flora International
4th floor, Jupiter House, Station Road,
Cambridge CB1 2JD
01223 571000
www.fauna-flora.org

Landlife (wildflower conservation)
National Wildflower Centre
Court Hey Park, Liverpool L16 3NA
0151 737 1819
www.landlife.org.uk

National Council for the Conservation of
Plants and Gardens
Home Farm, Loseley Park, Guildford GU3 1HS
01483 447540

National Garden Scheme Charitable Trust
Hatchlands Park, East Clandon, nr Guildford,
Surrey GR4 7RU
01483–211536
www.ngs.org.uk

Natural England
1 East Parade, Sheffield S1 2ET
enquiry service: 0845 600 3078
enquiries@naturalengland.org.uk
www.naturalengland.org.uk

Northern Ireland: Environment and Heritage Service
Klondyke Building, Cromac Avenue,
Gasworks Business Park, Lower Ormeau Road,
Belfast BT7 2JA
www.ehsni.gov.uk

Plantlife International
14 Rollestone Street, Salisbury, Wiltshire SP1 1DX
01722 342 730
www.plantlife.org.uk

Royal Horticultural Society
80 Vincent Square, London SW1P 2PE
0845 260 5000
membership enquiries: 0845 062 1111
www.rhs.org.uk

Scottish Natural Heritage
Great Glen House, Leachkin Road, Inverness IV3 8NW
01463 725000
www.snh.org.uk

Wales: Countryside Council for Wales
Maes-y-Ffynnon, Penrhosgarnedd, Bangor,
Gwynedd LL57 2DW
www.ccw.gov.uk

The Wildlife Trusts
The Kiln, Waterside, Mather Road, Newark NG241WT
01636 677711
www.wildtrusts.org

Index